Cyberspace and the State:
Toward a Strategy for Cyber-power

David J. Betz and Tim Stevens

Cyberspace and the State:
Toward a Strategy for Cyber-power

David J. Betz and Tim Stevens

IISS The International Institute for Strategic Studies

The International Institute for Strategic Studies

Arundel House | 13–15 Arundel Street | Temple Place | London | WC2R 3DX | UK

First published November 2011 by **Routledge**
4 Park Square, Milton Park, Abingdon, Oxon, OX14 4RN

for **The International Institute for Strategic Studies**
Arundel House, 13–15 Arundel Street, Temple Place, London, WC2R 3DX, UK
www.iiss.org

Simultaneously published in the USA and Canada by **Routledge**
270 Madison Ave., New York, NY 10016

Routledge is an imprint of Taylor & Francis, an Informa Business

DIRECTOR-GENERAL AND CHIEF EXECUTIVE John Chipman
EDITOR Nicholas Redman
ASSISTANT EDITOR Janis Lee
EDITORIAL Jeffrey Mazo, Jens Wardenaer, Ayse Abdullah
COVER/PRODUCTION John Buck

The International Institute for Strategic Studies is an independent centre for research, information and debate on the problems of conflict, however caused, that have, or potentially have, an important military content. The Council and Staff of the Institute are international and its membership is drawn from almost 100 countries. The Institute is independent and it alone decides what activities to conduct. It owes no allegiance to any government, any group of governments or any political or other organisation. The IISS stresses rigorous research with a forward-looking policy orientation and places particular emphasis on bringing new perspectives to the strategic debate.

The Institute's publications are designed to meet the needs of a wider audience than its own membership and are available on subscription, by mail order and in good book-shops. Further details at www.iiss.org.

Printed and bound in Great Britain by Bell & Bain Ltd, Thornliebank, Glasgow

British Library Cataloguing in Publication Data
A catalogue record for this book is available from the British Library

Library of Congress Cataloging in Publication Data

ADELPHI series
ISSN 1944-5571

ADELPHI 424
ISBN 978-0-415-52530-5

Contents

ACKNOWLEDGEMENTS

This is not a tactical playbook for cyberwar, let alone a technical work on operations in cyberspace. This is in very small part because we are strategists and social scientists, not cyberwarriors; but in large part because the literature on cyberspace already has many such works. It is intended as a strategic primer on the new reality of the Information Age, of which cyberspace is a preeminent part, for those who would elect to intervene in it or mould it to their advantage.

This book benefited greatly from the exchange of ideas generated in two workshops, funded by the Northrop Grumman Corporation, which took place in 2010. The workshops brought together policymakers, representatives of ICT industries, academics and lawyers to identify the key security issues pertaining to the cyber domain and to identify policy responses. The research for this title is part of the output of the US Defense Department's Minerva Initiative-funded project at King's College London, 'Strategy and the Network Society'. Their support is gratefully acknowledged.

Tim Stevens acknowledges the support of an Economic & Social Research Council scholarship (ES/H022678/1) funded under the RCUK Global Uncertainties Programme.

GLOSSARY

ARPANET	Advanced Research Projects Agency Network
APT	Advanced Persistent Threat agents
COIN	Counterinsurgency
CIA	Central Intelligence Agency, USA
GCHQ	UK Government Communication Head Quarters
ICANN	Internet Corporation for Assigned Names and Numbers
ISP	Internet service provider
IP	Internet protocol
IT	Information technology
ITU	International Telecommunication Union
MIT	Massachusetts Institute of Technology
NATO	North Atlantic Treaty Organisation
NIPRNet	Non-Classified IP Router Network (US Department of Defense)
OCSIA	UK Office for Cyber Security and Information Assurance
RICU	Research, Information and Communications Unit (UK)
SCO	Shanghai Cooperation Organisation
4GW	Fourth-Generation Warfare theory

Cyberspace has come a long way since its birth as a concept in science fiction in the early 1980s. Within three decades it has been defined in military doctrine as a new domain of conflict, while in broader societal terms it has come to be seen as the informational substrate in which whole economic ecosystems and industries grow. In developed states it touches most aspects of the lives of citizens, from the ways they make money and are governed, to how they build and maintain social relationships and find spiritual and intellectual sustenance. Although experts may differ on the details, in broad terms cyberspace may be said to possess these attributes and effects:

- it obscures the identity and location of actors because of its physical architecture and software protocols, which permit the relatively easy use of aliases and proxies that are relatively difficult to penetrate and reveal;
- it radically increases the speed, volume and range of communications, not just of powerful states and corporations, but also of individual citizens who can use it to communicate globally, almost instantaneously, with

reasonable security, using a variety of media from text to video. Although it is unevenly distributed – that is, omnipresent in some places but nonexistent in others – access is trending sharply upward across the world, including in the poorest regions where the telecommunications sector tends to be the fastest growing sector of the economy. The pace of proliferation is partly down to the democratic nature of the technology, which is another defining feature.

- The barriers to entry to cyberspace, such as they are, are lowering further with the spread of low-cost, Internet-enabled devices that combine voice communications, web-access and still and video photographic capabilities. The basic requirements for access are computers and data connection.

These combined attributes have great potential to disrupt the status quo, which is not a priori a bad thing. The historically unparalleled dense web of interconnected computers and people thus represents something of a paradox. It creates a wealth of opportunities for commercial enterprise and for the delivery of public goods and services, as well as new ways for citizens to participate in civil society; but it also creates awesome opportunities for the world's most sophisticated militaries and their various opponents, both state and non-state, to employ new ways and potentially powerful means of strategic action, which are arguably difficult to defend against and complex to deter. The UK's 2010 National Security Strategy, *A Strong Britain in an Age of Uncertainty*, captures this paradox of opportunity and vulnerability perfectly:

Britain today is both more secure and more vulnerable than in most of her long history. More secure, in the sense that we do not currently face, as we have so often in our past, a conventional threat of attack on our territory by a hostile power. But more vulnerable, because we are one of the most open societies, in a world that is more networked than ever before.[1]

In a 'networked society' – that is, one whose social structure is characterised by networks activated by information technology[2] – new elites derive their power from an enhanced ability to delve between the layers of hardware and software from which cyberspace is constructed. The power potential of non-state actors thus is substantially boosted. It is this apprehension that networked societies face threats which previous societal forms did not that pervades strategic writings on the topic. In its 2010 *National Security Strategy*, the US government warned that 'the very technologies that empower us to lead and create also empower those who would disrupt and destroy'.[3] Indeed, practically all developed states are asking how they must adapt to this new and confusing reality. Their sense of urgency in doing so is heightened by the way all manner of cyber-prefixed threats are splashed across the covers of popular books and newspapers. Critical national infrastructures are said to be vulnerable to cyber-attack; the vitality of the economy is said to be threatened with enervation through cyber-espionage and cyber-crime, which plunder intellectual property and threaten electronic commerce; and the property and well-being of citizens are claimed to be endangered by cyberwar. In June 2010, the incoming Defense Department chief Leon Panetta testified before the Senate Armed Services Committee that 'the next Pearl Harbor that we confront could very well be a cyber-attack'.[4]

We are in the midst of a 'cyber-scare', in which politicians and the media collude with IT security firms. The simple question, then, is how scared should we really be? Fortunately, this is not the first time such a societal shock has happened and we may learn from these previous instances. As author Bruce Sterling has observed:

> For the average citizen in the 1870s, the telephone was weirder, more shocking, more 'high-tech' and harder to comprehend, than the most outrageous stunts of advanced computing ... in the 1990s. In trying to understand what is happening to us today, with our bulletin-board systems, direct overseas dialling, fibre-optic transmissions, computer viruses, hacking stunts, and a vivid tangle of new laws and new crimes, it is important to realize that our society has been through a similar challenge before – and that, all in all, we did rather well by it.[5]

In general, consternation about cyberspace is perhaps best explained by communications theorist Marshall McLuhan, who observed in 1967 that 'wherever a new environment goes around an old one there is always new terror'.[6] The specifics of today's 'new terror' are of particular interest to us. Our argument is relatively straightforward: cyberspace alters much but it does not change everything and it changes things in the military sphere, which has traditionally preoccupied strategists, considerably less than has been supposed. Cyberspace has not had any single, overarching effect on all fields of human activity – cultural, economic and military. Perhaps the wisest counsel, therefore, is to seek some 'altitude' because, with a degree of distance, processes that appear existentially threatening at close hand can take on different hues.

In search of analytical high ground

Cyberspace is notoriously difficult to pin down. The term is widely used as an equivalent of the Internet or the World Wide Web; and generally in the public consciousness it is seen as a very new thing, seemingly coming from nowhere and exploding into ubiquity within a couple of decades. However, cyberspace is not to be confused with the Internet. The former is a metaphor, while the latter is composed of real hardware: a global network of computers using standard protocols to communicate with one another. Nor is it the same thing as the World Wide Web, the system of interlinked hypertext documents that are accessed via the Internet. Moreover, cyberspace is not all that new. We associate it with computer technology that has only relatively recently entered our homes; but in actuality it is a hybrid of telephones, television and computers, each with its own history and characteristics, which are in the process of converging. In other words, while cyberspace as a term is a mere 30 years old, cyberspace as the metaphorical 'place' in which machine-mediated communications occur is more than a century old; and cyberspace as a form of the public sphere has been with us since 1,000 BCE, when the citizens of Greek city states met for public debate and discussion in outdoor spaces called *agora*.

As strategists, therefore, as we try to comprehend the 'cyber threat' we must take care not to constrain our vision to the narrowly contemporary or to the merely technological. There are significant lessons to be learned from taking a broader historical and conceptual approach. Furthermore, so long as computers are non-sentient, it is from people that the 'cyber threat' principally emerges. The basis of cyber strategy is still the reciprocal interaction of human choice in conflict. Some things change, some stay the same. In one of the seminal early essays on cyberspace, John Perry Barlow captured a flavour of its simultaneous technical novelty and human familiarity which is worth quoting at length:

> To enter [cyberspace], one forsakes both body and place and becomes a thing of words alone. You can see what your neighbours are saying (or [what they] recently said), but not what either they or their physical surroundings look like. Town meetings are continuous and discussions rage on everything from sexual kinks to depreciation schedules.
>
> There are thousands of these nodes in the United States, ranging from PC clone hamlets of a few users to mainframe metros like CompuServe, with its 550,000 subscribers. They are used by corporations to transmit memoranda and spreadsheets, universities to disseminate research, and a multitude of factions, from apiarists to Zoroastrians, for purposes unique to each.
>
> Whether by one telephonic tendril or millions, they are all connected to one another. Collectively, they form what their inhabitants call the Net. It extends across that immense region of electron states, microwaves, magnetic fields, light pulses and thought which sci-fi writer William Gibson named Cyberspace.
>
> Cyberspace, in its present condition, has a lot in common with the 19th Century West. It is vast, unmapped, culturally and legally ambiguous, verbally terse (unless you happen to be a court stenographer), hard to get around in, and up for grabs. Large institutions already claim to own the place, but most of the actual natives are solitary and independent, sometimes to the point of sociopathy. It is, of course, a perfect breeding ground for both outlaws and new ideas about liberty.[7]

This is not to deny the rapidity of technological change in the last half century. The first electronic (as opposed to mechanical) computer, built in 1946 in order to calculate artillery firing tables for the US military, occupied a whole building on its own and was terrifically expensive.[8] A team of PhDs was needed to operate it. Transistor-based computers such as the IBM 1401, which came along 15 years later, were about the size of a large refrigerator and had a memory capacity of a few kilobytes. These were somewhat easier to operate and cost mere thousands of dollars per month to rent. The real tipping point came in the mid-1960s with the invention of the integrated circuit and subsequent advances in silicon-chip miniaturisation. Intel co-founder Gordon Moore was the first to apprehend where the historical trend was heading to 'such wonders as home computers, or at least terminals connected to a central computer, automatic controls for automobiles, and personal portable communications equipment'.[9] Microprocessor technology led to the wide availability of vastly more powerful, cheaper and more portable computers that surround us today.

The growth of the Internet has been similarly explosive. What began in 1969 with the Advanced Research Projects Agency Network (ARPANET), which linked computers at four American universities, has grown to global proportions driven by innumerable websites delivering ever greater amounts of commerce, entertainment and social networking. The 2011 CISCO *Visual Networking Index* predicts that, by 2015:

- annual global IP [Internet protocol] traffic will reach the zettabyte threshold (966 exabytes or nearly 1 zettabyte);[10]
- the gigabyte equivalent of all movies ever made will cross global IP networks every five minutes; and,
- the number of devices connected to IP networks will be double the global population.[11]

These are startling numbers, yet we should not lose sight of the fact that the purpose of all this traffic is to serve the need of humans to do what they have always done: communicate, collaborate, argue, not to mention consume and fight. We should bear in mind Barlow's sage observation that cyberspace is a breeding ground for 'outlaws' and 'new ideas of liberty'.

Rise and demise of the hacker

The new digital outlaws are, of course, hackers. A BBC report from June 2011 began with the definition: 'in the early decades of the 21st century the word "hacker" has become synonymous with people who lurk in darkened rooms, anonymously terrorizing the Internet.'[12] The current dark image of the hacker as a combination of vandal, thief, subversive and terrorist could hardly be further from that of the first hackers: the crewcut-and-short-sleeved young men of the MIT's Tech Model Railway Club in the late 1950s. As Steven Levy describes it in his highly regarded hacker history, a 'hack' in MIT usage was

> a project undertaken or a product built not solely to fulfil some constructive goal, but with some wild pleasure taken in mere involvement ... as the TMRC people used the word, there was serious respect implied ... to qualify as a hack, the feat must be imbued with innovation, style, and technical virtuosity.[13]

The first generation of hackers was essentially in it for the primal thrill of maximising code, their main interest being attaining technical mastery of the clunky early digital machines. One hacker described programming in vaguely spiritual terms as 'eerily transcendent'.[14]

Indeed, they possessed a 'hacker ethic', not laid out in a manifesto as such but nevertheless generally held in unspoken agreement among their community.[15] The ethic in many ways flowed from the logic of the computer itself; in Levy's words, 'it was a philosophy of sharing, openness, decentralization, and getting your hands on machines at any cost to improve the machines, and to improve the world'. These are attractive, even lofty principles; but in extremis, they amount to a self-licence to trespass and steal.

> Hackers believe that essential lessons can be learned about the systems [and] about the world from taking things apart, seeing how they work, and using this knowledge to create new and even more interesting things. They resent any person, physical barrier, or law that tries to keep them from doing this.[16]

In a similar vein, take the original hackers' bête noire, the thing standing between them and their beloved machines:

> Bureaucracies, whether corporate, government, or university, are flawed systems, dangerous in that they cannot accommodate the exploratory impulse of true hackers. Bureaucrats hide behind arbitrary rules (as opposed to the logical algorithms by which machines and computer programs operate): they invoke those rules to consolidate power, and perceive the constructive impulse of hackers as a threat.

For some hackers, it is not a great leap from a dislike of a specific bureaucracy to more general anti-establishment feelings. The first generation of hackers, however, did not make this leap. Their sins, best described as apolitical pranks, were directed at university administrators and many of their 'constructive impulses' really did better the world.

Nevertheless, from quite early on in the second generation of hackers, there was a connection between counter-culture and the emerging cyber-culture.[17] Stewart Brand – the founder of the 1960s hippie-classic *Whole Earth Catalog* who later co-founded the San Francisco-based WELL (for Whole Earth 'Lectronic Link), the first 'virtual community' – was one of those at the crux of this cultural cross-over. It was he who reformulated the original hacker ideal that information should flow freely, since this was more efficient in programming terms, into the slogan 'information wants to be free'. To this he added a substantial caveat:

> Information also wants to be expensive. Information wants to be free because it has become so cheap to distribute, copy, and recombine – too cheap to meter. It wants to be expensive because it can be immeasurably valuable to the recipient.[18]

Thus we may see that the 'hacker ethic' is in one sense essentially apolitical and technically focused, while in another it is subversive and profoundly ideological. This duality was not very meaningful in the days when the digital world was small and the knowledge required to operate in it so esoteric; in a world of very few computers, few or none owned by individuals, with few networks between them, cyberspace and 'real space' barely overlapped. However, as the number and power of computers and the networks between them expanded, hackers had a progressively larger 'canvas' on which to express themselves and ever more sophisticated and powerful means of doing so.

Generally, the first major penetration of the computer into the average household went unnoticed. In the mid-1960s the telephone companies started switching calls with computer exchanges instead of human operators or basic electromechanical systems. From the consumer's point of view little changed, but for the hackers a whole new digital world was opening to exploration. The third generation of hackers, or 'phone phreaks' (that is, phone hackers rather than computer hackers) to be precise, quickly cottoned on to the possibility of tricking telephone switching systems into granting free access to long-distance lines by mimicking the system's in-band signalling tone, a tone of 2,600 hertz.[19] To the telephone companies, phreaking was theft; phreaks, however, considered it illegal only in the sense that caving might be deemed illegal if AT&T owned all the caves. Two of the biggest and most mainstream names in computing today, Steve Wozniak and the late Steve Jobs, founders of Apple Computer, got their start selling 'blue boxes' (phone-tone generators needed for phreaking) in college dormitories.[20]

What really brought hacking into the public consciousness was the Hollywood movie *WarGames* (1983), in which a high-school student inadvertently brought the world to the brink of nuclear war when he hacked into a computer games company and infiltrated an experimental military supercomputer designed for nuclear war-gaming. Ultimately, he used a logic trap (a tic-tac-toe game) to convince the computer not to set off the Third World War. The film captured the public's fear of imminent nuclear war: President Ronald Reagan was reported to have sidetracked a briefing on the MX ballistic-missile programme with a detailed account of the film's plot, which had evidently intrigued him;[21] it was credited in federal legislation on computer crime as providing a 'realistic representation of the automatic dialling and access capabilities of the personal computer';[22] and Sergey Brin, co-founder of Google, at a 25th anniversary screening, described the film as 'a key movie of a generation, especially for those of us who got into computing'.[23]

To be sure, fiction had a certain head start on reality. In 1983 the Internet had only just evolved from the ARPANET and consisted of just a few hundred hosts.[24] Even so, it was not very long after digital networks became prevalent that groups and individuals came along to prey on them. In the early 1980s a large number of underground bulletin boards emerged with names like 'ShadowSpawn Elite', the 'Legion of Doom', and the 'Neon Knights'. The first group to attract the concentrated attention of the security services, however, was the '414s', a Milwaukee-based group of high-school hackers whose intrusions into the computers of the Sloan-Kettering Cancer Centre, Security Pacific Bank and Los Alamos National Laboratory caused a minor media storm in the summer of 1983. A *Time* magazine report from 1983 highlights the same dilemma that preoccupies security advisers in the *National Security Strategy* 30 years later.

> The Sloan-Kettering caper and this summer's hit movie *WarGames* ... have focused attention on a serious question: How to safeguard information stored inside computers? ... Many of these machines are hooked into the telephone system, which enables them to communicate with other computers and with users in remote locations. But as the 414s have demonstrated, anyone with one of the popular new microcomputers has the potential, however remote, to unlock the secrets contained in machines operated by banks, hospitals, corporations and even military installations.[25]

In short, the basic threat has long been known. What is not so clear is how, if at all, states might have been putting digital means to offensive use at the time. One occasionally cited example is the 1982 explosion of the Soviet Union's Urengoy–

Surgut–Chelyabinsk gas pipeline, which was allegedly caused by software rigged by the CIA. As the story goes, the pipeline required sophisticated computer control systems, which the Soviets could not themselves produce and therefore sought to obtain from the West. The software they obtained was said to have been altered at the manufacturing stage by the CIA introducing malicious code that caused the pumps, turbines and valves of the line to operate at settings that burst its joints and welds, causing an explosion equivalent to a small nuclear device. The blast was detected by US satellites. There is, however, no conclusive evidence that the CIA was involved in the incident. Russian sources deny sabotage took place, and there is no media report of the explosion. Declassified CIA accounts also make no mention of the incident.[26] Another widely reported military hack was alleged to have occurred during the 1991 Gulf War, when the United States is said to have attacked Iraqi military computer systems with a virus installed in a printer assembled in France and shipped to Iraq via Jordan. The virus reportedly disabled the Windows operating system of infected computers and took out their display and printer controllers. The incident was merely a hoax, an April Fool's story originally concocted in an English trade journal which was picked up by the Tokyo bureau of an American newspaper (somehow losing the joke in translation) and retransmitted into the American media as fact.[27]

Although it is difficult to ascertain what, if anything, states were doing in the realm of 'information warfare', by the mid-1990s there was a burgeoning literature speculating on the subject and outlining its dark potential. For example, in the introduction to *Cyberwar* (the first of several books with that title) it was proclaimed:

> information warfare has the side benefit for the attacker to create confusion, panic and irrationality

among the civilian target population, further contrib-
uting to the weakening of its 'will to fight'. It can be
applied surreptitiously, without massive destruction
of cities or other economic assets. Information warfare
aimed at the civilian information infrastructure may
be the next major innovation in the domain of strategic warfare.[28]

What is verifiable, however, often through court proceedings
and other documented accounts, are the activities of the third
generation of hackers who stalked the electronic byways of
telecoms networks, dial-up computer bulletin boards, and the
emerging strands of the World Wide Web in the 1990s. One of
the most interesting accounts of this generation is contained in
the book *Underground* by Suelette Dreyfus and Julian Assange
(later of WikiLeaks fame). In the introduction they described
some 'common themes' of the hacker profile:

> Rebellion against all symbols of authority.
> Dysfunctional families. Bright children suffocated
> by ill-equipped teachers. Mental illness or instability.
> Obsession or addiction.[29]

These common themes are significant, not least in the case of
the hacker 'Mendax', not revealed in the book as being the *nom
de guerre* of Assange himself.[30] As with previous generations,
there was the same curiosity and the thrill of the hack which
seems to have been the primary motivation:

> Hacking was the ultimate cerebral buzz for me ... It
> was a whole different world where there were no
> condescending adults and you were judged by your
> talent ... [When] I would start actually hacking ... my

brain would be going a million miles an hour and I'd basically completely forget about my body as I would jump from one computer to another trying to find a path into my target.[31]

But other motivations existed as well; the 'constructive impulse' soon manifested in destructive rebelliousness and sabotage. The first politically motivated computer 'worm' attack occurred in October 1989 on the eve of the launch of the *Galileo* space-probe, when NASA staff logged onto their computers to find this message on their screens:

WORMS AGAINST NUCLEAR KILLERS
WANK
Your System Has Been Officially WANKed
You talk of times of peace for all, and then prepare
for war.[32]

The worm then appeared to be deleting all the files on the infected computer. In actuality, the worm was not deleting files, it was merely causing heart palpitations amongst NASA's computer-systems officers. *Galileo* had attracted protest from the anti-nuclear movement because its space-bound electrical systems were powered by the radioactive decay of 24 kilograms of plutonium which, in the event of a crash, might have caused an Earth-bound ecological disaster. The worm was sophisticated, with a basic ability to learn, explore infected computers and propagate by copying itself through any open network connections; but it was also very simple: its rampage through NASA's systems used the most elementary attack strategy – username equals password.

It is tempting to think Assange was involved, though the evidence is circumstantial. His account of the attack in

Underground is highly detailed; it is known that it originated in Australia; and Assange/Mendax was one of the most accomplished hackers there at the time.[33] It would also fit with his view of the hacker community, which was described by one erstwhile colleague later in life as highly unusual:

> He thought they were 'useless' idiots ... He was always judging people on their 'usefulness', however he defined that category in a given situation. In his eyes, even particularly gifted hackers were idiots if they didn't apply their talents toward a larger goal.[34]

The larger goal in this case was clearly that of the anti-nuclear movement, which was adopted by an unnamed hacker. Moreover, in *Underground* Assange/Mendax is described as having a main aim of hacking into the Defense Department's National Information Center's main computer. Once he had penetrated the system, he was surprised to learn he had been beaten to it by US military hackers, apparently compromising their own security simply to highlight weaknesses (a practice known as Red Teaming), though they had apparently not made the administrators aware of the breach in security. Regardless of its authorship, the attack was by no means an 'operational success'; it caused about half a million dollars' worth of damage, but it did not stop the *Galileo* launch; and no one claimed credit for it in the end. What really worried computer security specialists was two-fold. Firstly, if NASA, one of the most technically sophisticated institutions anywhere, had such lax computer security that a 'computer-literate teenager could have cracked it wide open', then how badly secured was everyone else? Secondly, what might have been accomplished by a worm programmed by more seasoned specialists with seriously malicious intent?[35]

A hacker who has infiltrated a computer and gained administrator-level access to its systems has enormous power within that system; indeed, in hacker slang he 'owns' it. This does not require sophisticated equipment. There are many examples of hackers using quite simple equipment to control much more powerful systems: the phone phreaker known as 'Cap'n Crunch' (a.k.a. John Draper) earned his handle demonstrating that the 2,600hz tone needed for hacking telephone systems could be generated by the toy whistle found as a gift in a box of the breakfast cereal from which he took his name. What is done with that power depends on the sort of hacker possessing it.[36] Most, as 'Cap'n Crunch' protested, do nothing:

> If I do what I do, it is only to explore a System. Computers. Systems. That's my bag. The phone company is nothing but a computer.[37]

However, various hacker typologies exist, the most basic of which simply distinguishes between non-malicious ones ('white hats' or 'ethical hackers' exploring a system for their own enjoyment or testing its security on behalf of its owners) and malicious ones ('black hats' or 'crackers' breaking into a system for some other purpose). These other purposes are the key to further malicious hacker subtypes, such as 'grey hats' whose activities fall somewhere on the spectrum between these two poles.[38]

Cyber criminals, the largest category, are thieves using diverse and sometimes highly innovative techniques to steal. Like the transition from 'old school' hacking to 'phone phreaking', the move into cyber-crime (in particular 'carding', using a stranger's credit-card number to charge purchases) happened almost as soon the spread of electronic money transfers and credit made it possible.[39] 'Advanced persistent threat' (APT) agents (as cyber-security experts call them) are more sophisticated and well-organised groups operating out of a 'safe-harbour' country, targeting specific institutions for purposes of industrial espionage and intellectual property theft of long-term value. Corporate spies differ from them in not operating from a safe-harbour country; they are also usually less organised and more focused on targets of short- or mid-term value. What all these sorts of hackers have in common is that they hack for profit; whether as a personal enterprise or on behalf of a client (state or commercial), they hack for a living.

By contrast, 'hacktivist' groups such as 'Anonymous' and 'LulzSec' hack for fun (or 'lulz' in Internet slang) and out of some conviction, be it political, religious, environmental or personal. They have come to prominence with a string of high-profile attacks (typically website defacement and denial of service (DoS), but also theft of data such as e-mail records and customer information databases) on corporations such as Sony and HBGary, state targets (notably the United States Senate and CIA websites), and other institutions ranging from the Church of Scientology to the International Monetary Fund. One cyber crime analyst remarked of these incidents:

> These stunts are being pulled at the same time as national governments are wringing their hands about what to do in the event of a concerted network attack that takes out some critical infrastructure component ... It's not too hard to understand why so many people would pay attention to activity that is, for the most part, old school hacking – calling out a target, and doing it for fun or to make some kind of statement, as opposed to attacking for financial gain.[40]

Then there are the 'cyber warriors', hackers in state employ, sometimes in uniform, possibly acting in the manner of advanced persistent threat (APT) agents or corporate spies but doing so in the cause of specific policy objectives. Cyber warriors may also be employed to create and operate malware, such as the Stuxnet worm, which was thought by some to have been created jointly by the United States and Israel in order to attack Iran's nuclear programme.[41]

The most energetic cyber warriors (at any rate the ones at whom fingers are pointed most often) are said to be Chinese. Richard Clarke is at the forefront of those arguing that this amounts to a Chinese 'cyber-assault':

> China is systematically attacking the computer networks of the U.S. government and American corporations. Beijing is successfully stealing research and development, software source code, manufacturing know-how and government plans. In a global competition among knowledge-based economies, Chinese cyber operations are eroding America's advantage.[42]

The Chinese government, as Clarke points out, denies all charges, protesting that the attackers are either non-governmental Chinese hackers, other governments pretending to be China, or fictions of the United States or another country designed to stir up anti-Chinese feeling. Such denials strain credulity, in the face of increasing allegations of China-based hackers penetrating high-level computer systems in Europe, North America and Asia in recent years. Pentagon officials have long claimed that their computer networks have been targeted in a series of Chinese attacks collectively called *Titan Rain*. According to Major-General William Lord, director of information, services and integration in the US Air Force's Office of Warfighting Integration,

> China has downloaded ten to 20 terabytes [ten to
> 20 trillion bytes] of data from the NIPRNet (DoD's
> Non-Classified IP Router Network) ... They're looking
> for your identity so they can get into the network as
> you ... There is a nation-state threat by the Chinese.[43]

In January 2010, a highly sophisticated series of attacks on
at least 34 companies in the technology, finance and defence
sectors, dubbed *Aurora* by the Internet security firm McAfee,
was widely thought to have originated in China. According
to an insider at Google, the most prominent victim of the
attack, the data the hackers were after was not commercial in
nature but political, specifically access to the e-mail accounts
of Chinese human-rights activists. Google was able to determine 'definitively' that the attack originated in China and was
not the work of amateurs. Google is 'under attack all the time,
primarily via unsophisticated channels', according to a source
quoted by *Wired* magazine:

> I can't go into detail to demonstrate the level of
> sophistication, but [the company] doesn't use that
> term lightly, and it is quite deliberate ... This is truly,
> truly beyond the pale. The political nature of this and
> the attempt to monitor activists, not only in China but
> out of it, is chilling.[44]

Also in 2008–09, researchers from the Citizen Lab at the
University of Toronto discovered the existence of a malware-
based cyber-espionage network which they called *GhostNet*.
Consisting of at least 1,295 infected computers (30% of which
could be considered as 'high-value'), *GhostNet* was especially
prevalent on computer systems of the private offices of the
Dalai Lama and other Tibetan targets. Analysis found it to

be capable of removing files without the targets' knowledge; logging keystrokes as well as surreptitiously triggering web cameras and audio devices.[45] As for who was behind all this, in the words of the analysts who discovered it:

> The most obvious explanation, and certainly the one in which the circumstantial evidence tilts the strongest, would be that this set of high profile targets has been exploited by the Chinese state for military and strategic-intelligence purposes. Indeed, as described above, many of the high confidence, high-value targets that we identified are clearly linked to Chinese foreign and defence policy, particularly in South and South East Asia.[46]

That said, however likely it is that the Chinese state is responsible, it is not possible as a matter of absolute surety to say that is the case, as the authors of the *GhostNet* report are at pains to emphasise.[47] Moreover, the correct categorisation of such activity is not war, but rather espionage, a serious infringement of sovereignty and a source of friction between states, but not on the order of magnitude of war.

Russia, too, is frequently charged with being behind various politically motivated cyber-attacks. In late April 2007, Estonia was the target for cyber-attacks ranging from DoS attacks, to website defacement and massive e-mail and comments spam. It followed a decision by the country's authorities to move a Soviet war memorial from Tallinn city centre to a park on its outskirts, just a couple of weeks before the annual 9 May celebration of the Soviet victory over Nazi Germany. Estonia's Minister of Defence Jaak Aaviksoo claimed that

> the attacks were aimed at the essential electronic infrastructure of the Republic of Estonia ... All major

commercial banks, telcos, media outlets, and name servers – the phone books of the Internet – felt the impact, and this affected the majority of the Estonian population. This was the first time that a botnet threatened the national security of an entire nation.[48]

Aaviksoo told the *New York Times* 'it can effectively be compared to when your ports are shut to the sea' (that is, a naval blockade, an act of war).[49] Even these sharp assessments of the power of the cyber-attacks, however, were exceeded by those of Speaker of the Estonian Parliament Ene Ergma, who said:

> When I look at a nuclear explosion and the explosion that happened in our country in May, I see the same thing … Like nuclear radiation, cyberwar doesn't make you bleed, but it can destroy everything.[50]

The short Russo-Georgian War in August 2008 also involved the widespread use of cyber-attacks. Coming before the outbreak of actual fighting, these consisted of DoS attacks on Georgian government websites, and website defacement, most notably on the website of Georgian President Mikheil Saakashvili, where visitors were redirected to a site comparing him to Adolf Hitler. Subsequently, there were attacks on the routers supporting Internet traffic in and out of Georgia, aimed at severing the country's cyberspace links with the outside world. Instructions on how to ping flood (a form of DoS attack) and conduct other malicious hacking attacks on Georgian government sites were provided on a number of Russian websites and discussion forums.[51]

Strong claims have been made on the basis of these incidents. For one, that cyberwar is 'real' and capable of 'devastating' modern nations; for another, that it has already begun as nations 'prepare the battlefield ... hacking into each other's networks and infrastructures'.[52] But on closer examination, the evidence in support of these claims is rather equivocal. The damage done in Estonia and Georgia by cyber-attack was small. The online portals of Estonia's leading banks were crashed and online banking was unavailable for 90 minutes on 9 May and for two hours on 10 May. The e-mail system of the Estonian parliament was shut down for several days. But there was no loss of life or territory, no major damage and no serious disruption of critical services.[53] Georgia did lose lives and territory due to physical attack; but the effect of the cyber-attacks on it were inconsequential. If anything, Georgia had the better of the information campaign. When the Russian Army was in a position to roll its tanks into Tbilisi and physically seize the Georgian government, which it would have done in the previous era as veterans of the Prague Spring might aver, citizens responded not by turning out en masse in the time-honoured manner to dig anti-tank ditches; but by turning to the global mediaspace to build up a rampart of international public opinion against any further Russian advance, a gambit which proved successful.[54] One might conclude from the evidence, as Richard Clarke does, that

> the Russians, in fact, showed considerable restraint in the use of their cyber weapons ... probably [because they are] saving them for when they really need them, in a conflict in which NATO and the United States are involved.[55]

There is another, simpler theory: Russia took its best 'cyber-shot', and that was it. In any event, as with China, the Russian government vigorously denies responsibility for the attacks. To be sure, there is circumstantial evidence of the involvement of Russian authorities in directing (possibly sponsoring and paying) Russian youth groups to engage in hacking.[56] The physical and cyber-attacks appear to have been coordinated and complementary in the case of the Russo-Georgia War. But there is no conclusive proof of Russian state agency, nor even that they are preparing the battlefield.

The so-called attribution problem is often framed as a legal problem with unusual technical aspects (or vice versa), as may be seen in an analysis of the cyber-attacks on Georgia by NATO's Cooperative Cyber Defence Centre:

> From a legal point of view ... it is the general murkiness of this grey area – the lack of clear policies and procedures, the lack of direct evidence of the attacking entity's identity – that may make such 'grey area' attacks even more attractive. In such a perceived environment, by deliberately remaining below the threshold of 'use of force', an attacking entity may believe there is less likelihood of reprisal even if the attacker's identity is suspected.[57]

However true that is, we ought to recognise that this situation is not new in the abstract: the overarching problem is strategic, not legal.[58] The element of ambiguity which the attribution of cyber-attacker's identity seems to bring to the fore has always existed in military affairs: is it not the same interplay of chance and probability which was, for Clausewitz, the natural realm of the commander? Moreover, long before the arrival of cyberspace strategists have been preoccupied with the way war increasingly transcends neat divisions, defying categorisations between regular and irregular, state and non-state, and even war and peace. In 2003, for instance, the highly regarded Australian strategic thinker Michael Evans wrote that 'interconnectedness propelled by globalization and its handmaiden, the information revolution' had caused the international security system to 'split between a traditional twentieth-century, state-centred paradigm and new twenty-first-century sub-state and trans-state strata'.[59]

The transformation of hacking since the invention of the digital computer tells us a few things that are of use in the analysis of this split. Progressively, hacking has become more objectively purposeful. As the digital realm within which hacking could take place expanded and overlapped with the 'real' world, it absorbed some of the real world's multitudinous conflicts and movements, for better or worse. Criminals co-opted hackers for criminal purposes; governments co-opted them for purposes of state, including espionage and war; and hackers as human individuals have voluntarily attached themselves to all sorts of social movements and causes out of whim or conviction. Thus we have seen a multiplication of hacker types, each with its own attitudes toward the state, ranging from indifference through support to greater or lesser degrees of exasperation, alienation and hostility. The current characterisation of hacker as 'outlaw' is a caricature of a distinctive subtype, not a description of the whole.

Just as we ought not to demonise hackers, neither should we lionise them. For instance, while the *Irish Times* described the hacker Julian Assange tongue-in-cheek, 'with his halo of martyrdom, shield of truth and righteous sword at the ready', as a sort of freedom-of-information cartoon hero, in fact many people take the 'hacktivist as Robin Hood' paradigm seriously.[60] From its earliest days, cyberspace has been suffused by a latent ideology born of a mix of technical pragmatism and heartfelt desire to 'improve the world', the latter an ideal echoed in Google's informal company motto 'Don't be evil'. In practice, however, the web sometimes aggregates people's worst tendencies more than it does their best ones. Networked terrorism is a specific case in point; more generally though, it can be said that cyberspace makes it relatively easy to be 'evil'. Jaron Lanier, one of the most well-known web theorists, recently gave this ominous warning:

> I worry about the next generation of young people around the world growing up with Internet-based technology that emphasizes crowd aggregation, as is the current fad. Will they be more likely to succumb to pack dynamics when they come of age? The recipe that led to social catastrophe in the past was economic humiliation combined with collectivist ideology. We have the ideology in its new digital packaging, and it's entirely possible we could face dangerously traumatic economic shocks in the coming decades.[61]

These are salutary words which remind us that the object of more fully understanding the nature of power and its characteristics with respect to cyberspace goes beyond the jockeying of states in a simple zero-sum game. Moreover, the ideology to which he refers is not one of the conventional -isms; it is rather the 'ideology of violation' with which the Internet has become suffused.[62] Essentially, this holds that things which it is possible to steal deserve to be stolen, and the security of things that are guarded ought to be tested to destruction by those with sufficient technical nous to do so. In real-world terms it is a burglar's philosophy; in cyberspace terms it is a philosophy whose morality rests on the knife edge of the hacker's motives, be they white-hat, black-hat or grey-hat. Either way, it represents a significant challenge to states whose sovereignty and data security are in a state of constant skirmish with cyberspace challengers, whether they be state, non-state or quasi-state.

CHAPTER ONE

Power and cyberspace

In common with land, sea, air and space, cyberspace is now often designated as a strategic domain in its own right, but it is different from other domains in several respects, the most important of which is that it is the only environment that is entirely manmade. However we define cyberspace, we are confronted with its artificiality. If we take it to be an electronic 'space' between the devices we use to access it, such as computers and cell phones, this space only exists by virtue of the supporting infrastructure that allows it to do so. If we include this infrastructure in our definition of cyberspace, then we have a layer of human and machine communication resting atop a layer of machines made by humans. In either sense, cyberspace is entirely constructed by man, which is not an observation we can easily make of other domains, even taking into account their modification by humans. This is not to say that communications lack physicality: the currency of cyberspace exchange is information in the form of electrons, which are very much physical entities; but computer-mediated communications do not possess traditional dimensionality as do the physical objects we encounter elsewhere in our everyday lives.

There is little consistency between governmental defini-tions of cyberspace. The US *Cyberspace Policy Review* (2009), for example, defines cyberspace as the 'globally-interconnected digital information and communications infrastructure [that] underpins almost every facet of modern society'.[1] By contrast, the UK *Cyber Security Strategy* (2009) defines cyberspace as encompassing 'all forms of networked, digital activities; this includes the content of and actions conducted through digital networks'.[2] The Canadian *Cyber Security Strategy* (2010) defines cyberspace as 'the electronic world created by interconnected networks of information technology and the information on those networks'.[3] Australia's *Cyber Security Strategy* (2009) does not use the term 'cyberspace' at all, preferring 'Internet' instead.[4] Alternative terms are employed in non-Anglophone contexts, some of which have culturally specific meanings and emphases, with differing implications for users and govern-ments alike.[5] To other commentators, the term 'cyberspace' is either an anachronism or is redundant. Yet it persists and is arguably increasing in its global political currency. Science fiction writer William Gibson, who coined the term in a 1982 short story, later said of his creation: 'it seemed like an effec-tive buzzword ... evocative and essentially meaningless. It was suggestive but had no real semantic meaning, even for me'.[6] Almost 30 years later, the word has acquired substantial meaning, even if this varies between contexts and countries.

The issue of defining cyberspace is not trivial. What we decide to include or exclude from cyberspace has significant implica-tions for the operations of power, as it determines the purview of cyberspace strategies and the operations of cyber-power. As mentioned, there are two basic conceptions of cyberspace: a model that excludes infrastructure, and one that includes it.

The 'exclusive model' and its many variants tend to treat cyberspace as a metaphor for the 'space' between the hardware components of computer networks.[7] It is not a space in any traditional geographical sense, but the experience of being 'in' cyberspace is such that it possesses many of the attributes of physical space, if only by association and analogy.[8] These virtual environments are no less 'real' than the physical world and both can be considered as components of the 'actual' world.[9] Cyberspace is therefore the place on and beyond the screen, and the space in the wires and in the air, where human communications are performed through the transfer of bits. It exists too, in some sense, in the minds of users. The boundaries between the real and the actual are substantially blurred, but in this 'exclusive model' cyberspace is bounded by the infrastructure that enables it, rather than inclusive of it.

In contrast, the 'inclusive model' and its variants incorporate the infrastructure required to access the social space of cyberspace. The social layer is merely the uppermost layer of a stacked model of two or more layers. At its simplest, this model consists of a 'virtual' layer of information riding on a physical layer of hardware. A more developed model is provided by Martin Libicki's physical–syntactic–semantic model.[10] The physical layer is the 'hard' technological substrate of cyberspace, consisting of the machines and the networks into which they are assembled and across which they communicate. This is the layer of hardware and the signals that travel between devices in this layer. The syntactic layer consists of the software and protocols that format and structure digital electronic information and which control computer systems and networks. The uppermost semantic layer contains the information exchanged, stored and otherwise manipulated in computer networks, usually by humans in the form of natural language or approximations thereof, and may otherwise be expressed as the layer in which meaning is extracted from information.

Although cyberspace is often characterised through the use of network terminology, it can also be thought of as a 'global fluid', which is also an inclusive terminology. While global fluids may operate through networks, many of which are indeed global, the metaphor of fluid applies better to the concept of cyberspace than does the network metaphor alone. Global fluids are 'partially structured by ... the networks of machines, technologies, organizations, texts and actors that constitute interconnected nodes along which flows [of capital, ideas, social energies, etc] can be relayed'.[11] Crucially, these fluids do not respect established morphological and social boundaries and 'may escape, rather like white blood corpuscles, through the "wall" into surrounding matter and effect unpredictable consequences upon that matter'.[12] This non-linearity means that a global fluid like cyberspace cannot simply be dismantled like a house or a car, nor can its parameters be easily traced, nor its behaviour readily predicted: cyberspace is in a state of constant flux. Neither a wholly social, nor a narrowly mechanistic view of cyberspace sufficiently captures its operations and experiences in the round. At all times, cyberspace is an assemblage of multiple actors, whose relations are never permanently stabilised.

One important implication of the differing perspectives above relates to what and whom we consider to be actors in cyberspace. Many of the current concerns expressed by governments are due to the proliferation of actors in cyberspace. States are obviously important actors and will continue to be so, but their online presence competes for influence with a wide range of entities who embrace the opportunities of cyberspace for their own purposes. These range from individual citizens to civil society organisations and commercial enterprises, from terrorists and insurgents to branches of state power (militaries, intelligence agencies, etc.) to multilateral global institutions and media conglomerates, from individual nodes to whole networks, and non-humans in the form of hardware and software too. Each seeks to use cyberspace to pursue its own ends, whether these be individually or in concert with others. Power is present in their mutual interactions, and asymmetries abound that expose power in its multifaceted forms, serving variously to empower or disempower actors.

The advent of global cyberspace has had a fundamental effect on how these actors interact. In cyberspace, any two actors are connected in time by only a few milliseconds, the time it takes for digital electronic communications to travel from one to the other, almost anywhere in the world. This is what the US military and others call 'netspeed'. Netspeed is nearly light-speed and to all intents and purposes collapses spatial distance to zero.[13] Spatial distance is in fact only sometimes discernible by the 'lag' that occurs in communications between one actor and another, such as may be experienced across slower Internet connections. The simultaneity of cause and effect in cyberspace has obvious ramifications for the exercise of some forms of power: actions initiated in one location can have instantaneous effects in another, regardless of their geographical separation. While this allows state actors access to a greater range of globally distributed targets amenable to coercion of various forms, it also facilitates the reverse dynamic, in which spatially distant others – particularly those outside a state's immediate jurisdiction – can exercise power against the wishes of a state with little or no chance of being traced or interdicted by that state. The reduction of time and space into instantaneous connection increases the number of actors that may be affected by forms of power that were previously constrained by physical and temporal separation. This dynamic affects all actors, regardless of their relative historical access to power.

In addition, the presence of ever-greater numbers of actors in cyberspace means intermediaries are also multiplying, who may or may not have any stake or immediately sensible role in the operations of state power. One way to illustrate why this is problematic is to revisit the philosopher Bertrand Russell's statement that power may be viewed as 'the production of intended effects'.[14] This remains the prevailing perception of strategists, for whom strategy is the art of unlocking the power inherent in national capacities to effect outcomes in the national interest in contest with other strategists acting in their own national interests. Russell's assertion may resonate with many who view power through the lens of direct cause and effect, but this picture is complicated by the character of cyberspace.

In global cyberspace, the interdependence and interconnectedness of massively networked users and devices irrevocably alters the traditional dynamics of cause and effect. Instead of being able to trace mechanically the passage of ideas and images through the nodes and linkages of older networks, in the 'new media ecology', 'nobody knows *who* will see an event, *where* and *when* they will see it or *how* they will interpret it', for example.[15] This means that the effects of power in cyberspace may be as unintended as they are intended. In the case of non-state actors, many of these might become the unintended casualties of power were it, for example, to be exercised irresponsibly or without due consideration to the possibilities of collateral damage. In 2008, for example, more than 300 civilian servers in Saudi Arabia, Germany and the US were compromised as a result of US military actions against a single CIA–Saudi 'honeypot' website deemed complicit in facilitating foreign fighters' passage to combat operations in Iraq.[16]

The publication of sensitive documents by WikiLeaks also illustrates the unintended effects of actions mediated through cyberspace, as these events, particularly the release of diplomatic cables beginning in November 2010, had many knock-on effects that could be described as non-linear in their unpredictability. Not least of these unexpected outcomes was the response of online 'hacktivists' like the Anonymous collective, who took it upon themselves to retaliate to the perceived harassment and surveillance of WikiLeaks members and associates by the US government and its commercial and security allies.[17] The effects of state and non-state actions in this case were experienced inside and outside cyberspace, and this speaks to the fact that cyberspace cannot be separated from the rest of the 'real' world. Power reaches into, out of and through cyberspace, as the social relations through which it is enacted and constructed are not confined to cyberspace alone.

Almost by definition, those human actors we encounter in cyberspace are representations (or avatars) of physical beings located elsewhere. While our social relations with them in cyberspace – if we slay them in simulated battle, or engage them in online debate, for example – might appear contained solely within cyberspace, this is not quite the case. Intentionally or otherwise, power relations in cyberspace extend to the physical world and affect human behaviours there too. It may also be the case that actions in cyberspace are deliberately intended to produce effects elsewhere. By the same token, actions outside cyberspace often produce effects inside it.[18]

It could even be argued that the majority of the effects of power mediated by cyberspace are experienced outside it, even if only in a secondary or attenuated sense. Social relations always begin and end outside cyberspace, even if their mediation is performed through a complex of machine actors, software and digitised avatars. In this sense, there are perhaps very few actors who do not have a primary physical manifestation, even if the locations where they communicate with others are entirely virtualised. Care therefore needs to be taken when we consider where actors are located and where the effects of power are experienced.

From power to cyber-power

The commonplace understanding of power is as a capacity or attribute with which an actor is endowed, or as a resource to be exploited to achieve particular ends. We are said to have or possess the power to do certain things, to alter the lives of other persons, to influence the minds of others, in essence to have a capacity, however gained, to wield power for one's own purposes and aggrandisement, often to someone else's detriment. Such usage, despite its ubiquity, has a paradoxical tendency to mystify power while purporting to explain exactly that which it often aims to critique, such as imbalances in access to resources, money, influence and personal prospects. Hiding within our common-sense use of power is a rather more banal but crucial observation: that power is only produced through the interactions of social beings, and has no existence outside of social action. Power does not exist without the relationships through which it is manifest. The operations of power may release the potency of an actor's capabilities, but without social interaction these capabilities may as well not exist. Power is not inherent, but must be somehow produced, and it is only made apparent by the effects it has on others. All power can therefore be characterised as 'the production, in and through social relations, of effects on actors that shape their capacity to control their fate'.[19]

Within politics and strategy, the predominant conception of power is one of direct coercion. This view owes an intellectual debt to Max Weber, who defined power as 'the chance of a man or of a number of men to realize their own will in a communal action even against the resistance of others who are participating in the action'.[20] The most relevant and commonplace definition of this form of power is that in which 'the central intuitively understood meaning of [power is where] ... A has power over B to the extent that he can get B to do something that B would not otherwise do'.[21] From this intuitive concept of power stems the idea that power is the ability of one state to marshal its resources in order to promote its interests against the interests of another. Resources in this context have tended to mean the quantifiable material assets of the state, such as land, population, raw materials and military forces. It is the task of strategy to use military resources to effect political change. As Lawrence Freedman writes, 'it takes strategy to unleash the power inherent in this [military] capacity and to direct it towards specific purposes'.[22] Strategy is therefore the creation and manipulation of social relations that allows for the exercise of national resources towards a common goal.

In recent years, the term 'cyber-power' has become more common in security and strategy discourse and is likely to gain even greater currency in the near future. Any use of the word 'power' with an environmental modifier like 'cyber' can only be a subjective one; it does not illuminate the core nature of power, except to connote that power operates in 'cyber' environments, as it does anywhere else where social relations occur. In this sense, cyber-power is part of a terminological lineage that includes 'airpower' and 'seapower' to describe the operations of national, principally military, coercive power in particular environmental domains. Cyber-power is therefore analogous to US airman William 'Billy' Mitchell's famous formulation of airpower as 'the ability to do something in the air'.[23] Military cyber-power – if we define it as the use, or threatened use, of cyberspace and other resources to effect strategic aims in and through cyberspace against the resistance or wishes of others – exemplifies this form of power.

However, we wish to widen the conception of cyber-power to include all forms of power in which power relations occur wholly or in part in or through cyberspace. The use of the prefix 'cyber' here does not fall into the trap of imparting either an unwarranted sense of 'glamour' or 'hype' to our discussion, as others have alleged of its use elsewhere.[24] Rather, cyber-power can be understood as the variety of powers that circulate in cyberspace and which shape the experiences of those who act in and through cyberspace.[25] This is consistent with our desire to address the grand strategic rather than merely the strategic. Cyber-power 'is not created simply to exist, but rather to support the attainment of larger objectives ... across the elements of national power – political, diplomatic, informational, military, and economic'.[26]

None of this is to suggest that cyber-power is a distinctive form of power in and of itself. Although the specific circumstances in which cyber-power operates are indeed different from, for instance, airpower or seapower, the forms of cyber-power described here share fundamentally similar features to the operations of power in other domains. By means of an example, the application of military force in war is always, as Clausewitz reminds us, an act of force to compel our enemy to do our will.[27] In this sense it is a very specific form of coercive power. Yet in its operations, coercive power takes on distinct characteristics depending on whether it is fought on land or at sea. The environment affects how power is mediated and what its specific effects are. It changes how social relations are constructed and manipulated but does not alter the essential dynamics of those social relations. Cyber-power is therefore the manifestation of power in cyberspace rather than a new or different form of power. This is an important caveat that can be similarly applied to the allied concepts of sovereignty, war and dominion. Local circumstances may produce novel events and peculiarities, but the same general principles apply. There are four basic forms of power whose operations can be seen in cyberspace as four distinct forms of cyber-power.[28]

Compulsory cyber-power

The first form of cyber-power is the use of direct coercion by one cyberspace actor in an attempt to modify the behaviour and conditions of existence of another. This form is therefore compulsory in the sense of compelling another to do our will. Coercion can also be exerted by non-state actors and compulsory cyber-power can be found in the interactions between non-state actors and states, and between non-state actors. Even if current hyperbole about 'cyberwar' is somewhat misplaced, forms of cyber conflict commonly occur and the state is only one of various actors involved.[29] The cast list is familiar: activists, hackers, criminals, terrorists, states, state proxies, military alliances, private firms, public companies and so on. Any actor with access to cyberspace and the requisite skills and knowledge can, hypothetically, enact compulsory cyber-power against another.

For example, the highly successful attack by the Internet group Anonymous on the data security and malware response company HBGary Federal showed one non-state actor exerting compulsory cyber-power against another. The firm was targeted after its CEO announced that the company had infiltrated Anonymous, discovered its members' real names and was going to publish them. In return, Anonymous hacked the firm's servers, defaced its website, downloaded tens of thousands of its corporate e-mails and posted them on the web, digitally harassed its CEO and other staff, and left a threatening note in the company's booth at the RSA security conference in San Francisco, which caused the cancellation of the launch announcement for a major new software product. As Vice-President Jim Butterworth put it: 'They decided to follow us to a public place where we were to do business and make a public mockery of our company.'[30] The company's CEO was ironically reduced to pleading, in vain, that his e-mail records not be released.[31]

Often, the immediate aim of a coercive action is to control the behaviour of a machine or network of machines, in order to change the behaviours of an individual or collective human actor. Direct control over remote machines modifies the range of options available to a given actor. It may also alter the conditions of an actor's existence to such a degree that an actor may no longer be able to go online, and is effectively disbarred from operating in cyberspace at all. These technical capabilities are being developed in dozens of countries, some of whom are extremely sophisticated operators in this environment. The same is true of those non-state actors who exploit the low barriers to entry to cyberspace in order to exercise cyber-power over elements of state apparatus in coercive and potentially damaging ways. Fears of such events underpin governments' concerns about 'cyber-doom scenarios'.[32]

Compulsory cyber-power also includes, in addition to the types of operations to which we have alluded above, the deployment of non-material resources in order to directly affect the actions of others. Symbolic resources, such as the threat of military action or economic coercion, should also be considered as negative sanctions available as tools of coercive cyber-power. These examples are closely tied to the deterrent and compellent effects strongly implied in, for example, the UK's *Cyber Security Strategy*, which talks of the desire to reduce 'an adversary's motivation and capability'.[33] Since such effects would only derive if actors recognise that resources have been arrayed against them and believe the credibility of threats made against them, it is highly likely that these types of compulsory cyber-power may be hard to implement.[34]

Institutional cyber-power

A second form of cyber-power involves the indirect control of a cyberspace actor by another, principally through the mediation of formal and informal institutions. The intermediary institution is not under the total control of a specific state actor. If it is, it should be considered as an agent of compulsory power. Institutional power exists when an actor is able to influence the ways in which intermediary institutions work such that it 'guides, steers, and constrains the actions (or nonactions) and conditions of existence of others'.[35]

Within cyberspace, state resources can be used to 'set norms and standards' of a variety of institutions impacting upon users' behaviour. Cyberspace can also be used to influence the opinions of foreign audiences through media institutions.[36] In recent years, the US has attempted to keep control of the Internet Corporation for Assigned Names and Numbers (ICANN), which manages the allocation of domain-name space on the Internet and is therefore at the heart of maintaining global network operability. Although presented as a 'bottom-up', non-governmental entity based in the US, it remains under the purview of the US government, specifically the Department of Commerce.[37] The US government attempts to influence the operations of this institution for its own economic ends, an obvious instance of institutional cyber-power. Similarly, the US is encouraging a soft form of 'cyber deterrence' through various global institutions by promoting normative and behavioural change in the 'rules of the road' for cyberspace.[38] Although there are many who agree with the US stance on these issues, there are those who do not, particularly China and Russia, who are effecting their own institutional cyber-power. They exercise this power through the International Telecommunication Union (ITU) and the Shanghai Cooperation Organisation (SCO), which they use to promote their national interests in the field of global Internet governance.

At the sub-state level, cyber-security practices provide another example of institutional cyber-power. In the UK, one of the managerial responsibilities of the Office for Cyber Security and Information Assurance (OCSIA) is an 'Awareness and Cultural Change' workstream, which requires it to 'identify and instil the changes in behaviour and working culture that our dependence on the cyber environment demands'.[39] One of the specific areas in which culture change is deemed necessary is that of information assurance. In this we see the operation of institutional power through intermediaries, whose task is in part to change the behaviours not only of technicians and information-security professionals, but also of government employees and companies with respect to ensuring the secure passage and storage of economically and politically sensitive data. A wide range of governmental and non-governmental organisations is actively engaged in this project. The use of the latter is an example of institutional cyber-power, ultimately coordinated by the state but articulated through a body of intermediaries able to effect change where the liberal state cannot. This element of the UK cyber-security project is as much a normative one as it is a practical one.

Structural cyber-power

Structural power works to maintain the structures in which all actors are located and which, to a large degree, permit or constrain the actions they may wish to take with respect to others with whom they are directly connected.[40] In this formulation, we are more concerned with how cyberspace helps determine these structural positions than with how the resulting actors shape cyberspace per se, as is the case with coercive and institutional cyber-power. Although it is probably not possible to conclude that cyberspace does any one thing with respect to international order, a starting point is to ask whether cyberspace perpetuates existing structural forms or facilitates the creation of new ones.

Scholars have long noted the transition of industrial economies to post-industrial ones based on the commodification of data, information and knowledge.[41] The concept of the 'informational society' is closely linked to that of networks, such that 'one of the key features of informational society is the networking logic of its basic structure, which [leads to] the concept of "network society"'.[42] Many authors have linked the rise of networks to the globalisation of capital and to the transformation of capitalism. Rather than entering an entirely new era of social organisation, as some terms like the 'Information Age' might suggest, it would be more accurate to state that the organisational form of capitalist society is transforming, but not beyond all recognition. Information technologies have changed much but they have not changed everything.[43]

The competitive logic of capitalism is reproduced through transformed structures of cognitive, cooperative and communicative labour mediated to a large degree by cyberspace, in which the goods and services are often located and even consumed, as in the case of downloaded music or film files, financial products and commercial data.[44] Although capitalism has been transformed in the 'network society', the relative structural positions of capital and labour are preserved, albeit in networked form. Structural power is manifest in these networks as much as it was during the Industrial Age.

Yet the networked form does offer something novel, if not entirely new.[45] Civic networks, structured around the tools, opportunities and forums of cyberspace, can outflank and on occasions replace the hierarchical structures of the industrial period. The Internet, in particular, is 'a global electronic agora where the diversity of human disaffection explodes in a cacophony of accents', such is the ability of online networks to organise and mobilise resistance activities, ostensibly beyond the reach of states and their sluggish bureaucracies and systems of control.[46] The events of the 2011 Arab Awakening have shown how the Internet can be used to motivate and mobilise citizens and how governments have moved to suppress such activities. Although we should not ascribe undue significance to the role of the Internet in effecting regime change, it is apparent that use of the Internet and other elements of cyberspace was an important factor in getting networks of concerned citizens to display publicly their opposition to incumbent governments in North Africa and the Middle East. These networks developed as people with their own forms of 'networked individualism' coalesced around points of preference and political projects that reflected their personal interests and values.[47] Nodes – that is, individuals and the points where they coalesce – within these structures may therefore be empowered to act in ways that would be impossible were it not for cyberspace, while remaining disempowered relative to the dominant economic system. Structural cyber-power therefore works both to maintain the status quo and to disrupt it.

Productive cyber-power

Cyberspace, as a quintessentially informational environment, is ideally suited to the performance and transmission of a productive cyber-power. This is the constitution of social subjects through discourse mediated by and enacted in cyberspace, which therefore defines the 'fields of possibility' that constrain and facilitate social action.[48]

Cyberspace serves to reproduce and reinforce existing discourses, as well as to construct and disseminate new ones. In many ways, productive cyber-power is the foundation for other forms of cyber-power: without constructed social beings there are no social relations through which power may manifest. Productive cyber-power also connects the military and political realms in war and aims to mould discourse to the advantage of the strategic actor.[49] This is particularly apparent in the use of 'soft' power to win hearts and minds, either during conflict, or before it. In an inclusive model of cyberspace, the 'uppermost' semantic layer is the principal space in which political struggles are manifest. In an era of 'strategic communication' and 'public diplomacy', productive cyber-power is perhaps the most important form of cyber-power.

One of the more obvious examples of how states demonstrate productive cyber-power is through the discursive construction of cyberspace threat actors. By identifying certain actors as threats to national security, states can pursue policies and strategies designed to treat them as legitimate targets of other forms of state power. The term 'hacker', for example, has altered significantly since its roots in the 1950s and 1960s. Now, hackers are far more likely to be portrayed as 'anti-social, possibly dangerous individuals', wreaking havoc on computer systems, rather than 'heroes' largely responsible for innovations driving the Internet and the World Wide Web.[50] Indeed, in many cases they are held to be 'the new enemy of the Information Age ... bad actors in the new social reality' of cyberspace.[51]

Although some hackers are anti-social and destructive, many are simply inimical to the designs and ethos of the state system and demonised accordingly. In late 2010, much was made of WikiLeaks figurehead Julian Assange's background as a hacker. In one international magazine article describing Assange's past, the standfirst 'Crusader, Hacker, Megalomaniac, Extortionist', left little doubt as to his conjectured moral status.[52] As with much else in cyberspace, this category is not fixed, and recent government overtures to 'ethical' hacker communities have been based on offers of employment rather than threats of arrest.[53] In this context in the UK, hackers were glossed as 'slightly naughty boys' by then Security Minister Lord West.[54] The moral dichotomy between 'ethical' and 'unethical' is further emphasised by the opposing terms 'white hat' and 'black hat' hacker, respectively.

Cyberspace is a potent medium of productive power expressed through the promotion and dissemination of existing and emerging narratives and worldviews. This applies as much to the state-centric narratives of 'soft power' as it does, for example, to jihadi web forum discourse. Both presume access to truths about theirs and others' status in the world; both meet resistance from those whom they would cast as 'other' or otherwise disempower. At its extremes there is little difference, for example, between dehumanising rhetoric regarding the inhabitants of Fallujah, in Iraq prior to *Operation Phantom Fury*, and the dehumanising rhetoric about *kufr* (non-believers) in jihadi discourse.[55] Both serve, among constituencies of the like-minded, to legitimise the killing of innocent people and allow for the development of strategies to do so, through the production of 'expedient discursive effects'.[56] Both are mediated by cyberspace, whether it is the *New York Post* or *Ansar al-Muja-hideen*.[57] They are also 'mediatised', in the sense that these platforms are not only channels of reportage but are complicit in the performance of conflict. The media of cyberspace are not a 'neutral middle-ground', however we parse their origins or organisation, from the grassroots to the multinational.[58]

The forms of cyber-power described above do not operate in isolation from one another. Indeed, it would be unusual if they did. Power is best conceived as a 'family' of related dynamics that, while distinct in and of themselves, interact to form what we generally describe as 'power'. It follows that cyber-power is not a monolithic concept: it has many parts, not all of which are necessarily present in any given event or process, nor which appear the same to all eyes. The authoritarian state perception of cyber-power will be very different to that of the pro-democracy activist in that same state, for example, even if in their interactions the same modes of power may be operating. When we wish to examine the operations of power in cyberspace, we need to consider the actual or possible presences of all forms of power, without which any conception of cyber-power must be incomplete.

State power, while normally viewed as a form of compulsory power, also has other facets determining the status of actors and the structures in which they are situated. State cyber-power should be viewed similarly: states may consciously pursue their interests in and through cyberspace through the operations of compulsory and institutional cyber-power, but strategists would be wise to consider the operations of structural and productive cyber-power in order, particularly, to better grasp the unintended effects that may occur, the ways in which actors are constructed and maintained, and the ways that ideas circulate and take hold. Only a rounded treatment of the various forms of cyber-power will provide a proper grounding for further considerations of what might constitute national cyber-power as an integral component of national strategy.

CHAPTER TWO

Cyberspace and sovereignty

Globalisation and technological transformation have long been heralded as the harbingers of the decline of states and state sovereignty. Writing in 1996, globalisation scholar Arjun Appadurai asserted that 'the nation-state, as a complex modern political form, is on its last legs'.[1] Former French diplomat Jean-Marie Guéhenno argued that the fundamental changes wrought by globalisation meant that traditional notions of the nation-state may well not survive long into the twenty-first century.[2] On present showing, however, the state is far from in decline, although the challenges it faces are increasingly evident and urgent. What have occurred in response to concerns about the effects of globalisation and innovation are changes in the national social, political and economic order.[3] It may also be true, as suggested by journalist Martin Wolf, that what has also passed in recent years is the 'delusion of the state's omnipotence' with respect to its ability to control global flows of information, persons and capital.[4]

Discussions of the effects of cyberspace on state sovereignty have tended to follow a broad narrative that describes the erosion of sovereignty as an inevitable consequence of global information exchange and the diminishing relevance of physical territory in cyberspace. Often held to be paradigmatic of this view is cyberspace theorist and activist John Perry Barlow's 1996 'Declaration of the Independence of Cyberspace'. In this e-mailed missive to friends and colleagues, and consciously adopting a Jeffersonian tone, Barlow addressed the governments of the industrialised world on behalf of the denizens of cyberspace: 'You are not welcome among us. You have no sovereignty where we gather.'[5] Barlow claimed to be building a new community in cyberspace – 'the new home of Mind' – replete with its own norms and internal regulatory practices, into which governments were neither invited nor deemed necessary. In this formulation, cyberspace was inherently 'anti-sovereign'. Although he has since observed wryly of his manifesto that it was embarrassing and hastily conceived,[6] Barlow's appeal to the libertarian and utopian instincts of many cyberspace users persists and speaks to the fundamental idea that territoriality (or lack thereof) has significant effects on the concept of sovereignty.

Unlike power, which is usually held to be fundamental to social interaction and constitution, sovereignty is a concept wholly derived from politics. If power is immanent to political relations, sovereignty is contingent upon the prevailing political theories and practices of the time, although it tends to a greater or lesser degree to encapsulate the idea that there is, or should be, a supreme authority within a territorial political entity.[7] As such, it is open to negotiation and liable to change, even if our perceptions of what sovereignty actually means tend to crystallise around assumptions particular to any given period of world history. In the modern era, sovereignty is closely linked to the nature of the state, without which sovereignty in its usual sense cannot be said to exist.[8] However, the supreme authority internal to the sovereign state has been circumscribed in the twentieth century by international norms such as human rights and proscriptions against genocide, and by supranational institutions such as the United Nations and the European Union. In the latter example, EU member-states 'pool' their sovereignty rather than dispense with it, but through this their supreme authority within their own borders is constrained.[9]

Sovereignty has been described as the 'master variable of the international system' in the eyes of International Relations scholars concerned with the actions and intentions of states.[10] Yet, as Robert Keohane has observed, sovereignty is more often discussed than it is defined.[11] Consequently, these discussions have tended towards analysis and opinion in which the term 'sovereignty' is used in multiple and inconsistent ways. In an attempt to restore some clarity to this situation, Stephen Krasner has argued that there are four ways in which 'sovereignty' is understood by scholars and others concerned with the conduct of states in the international system: domestic sovereignty, interdependence sovereignty, international legal sovereignty and Westphalian sovereignty.[12]

Domestic sovereignty is closely associated with the mainstream heritage of Western political philosophy. It is concerned with the organisation of public authority within states and the abilities of domestic authorities to make policy and regulate behaviour effectively. Domestic sovereignty therefore entails both authority and control, two concepts Krasner is keen to disentangle, and which do not occur together in any of the other three forms of sovereignty. Interdependence sovereignty concerns the ability to control the flows of people, materials, ideas and diseases across territorial boundaries. International legal sovereignty refers to the principle of states' mutual recognition of one another's independence as free and equal members of an international community of states. It is a matter of authority rather than control. Westphalian sovereignty is concerned with states having the right to determine their internal decision-making processes to the exclusion of external sources of authority. The various forms of sovereignty interact with one another and are also subject to various 'modalities of compromise' that constitute deviations from established norms and rules of sovereignty. Far from being exceptional, these compromises occur so regularly that Krasner perceives the working of sovereignty to be one of 'organised hypocrisy'.[13]

Each of these forms of sovereignty may be considered in relation to cyberspace; and it is incorrect to assume that cyberspace necessarily erodes sovereignty in all its forms. Cyberspace has almost no effect on international legal sovereignty, for example, yet it has important implications for the closely allied concept of Westphalian sovereignty. The most significant impact of cyberspace is on interdependence sovereignty, due to the transnational nature of information flows. This in turn has the potential to affect domestic sovereignty, and there are many examples of how this is indeed already happening. Yet even in this latter case, governments are using diverse methods to reassert domestic sovereignty through the instigation of technical controls and normative regimes, which themselves have necessarily transnational aspects and implications.

International legal sovereignty and cyberspace

International legal sovereignty is concerned with the establishment of political entities in the international system, through which they are recognised by other states as equal in international law, and through which their representatives are accorded familiar privileges such as diplomatic immunity and the opportunity to appear on the world stage.[14] Cyberspace offers no direct challenge to the integrity of international legal sovereignty as a source of authority. It has been neither the locus nor the conduit of serious attempts to subvert or otherwise exploit international legal sovereignty, although there have been attempts – one practical, one theoretical – to acquire international legal sovereignty for entities previously unrecognised by the international system.[15]

Since 1967, the owners of an abandoned Second World War sea fort in British territorial waters have asserted its status as the independent sovereign state of Sealand.[16] Their claims of de facto sovereignty are not supported by any other state and there are no signs that they ever will be. Nevertheless, since 2000, there have been several attempts to use Sealand as an offshore data haven, most publicly by Swedish file-sharing website The Pirate Bay in 2007.[17] By doing this they were aiming to circumvent existing data regulation by basing servers in locations with weak enforcement regimes. The Pirate Bay saw a potential opportunity to avoid incoming Swedish laws limiting copyright infringement by relocating its servers to the offshore location of Sealand, although the project was eventually abandoned. Such data havens may yet exist, but it is highly unlikely that they would be granted international legal sovereignty in the current international system, particularly given the climate of concern about unregulated data storage and exchange.

Rather more robust is the claim by some theorists and activists that cyberspace itself should be recognised as a sovereign entity in the international political system. These rely on statements of the unique nature of cyberspace, particularly with reference to its lack of traditional territorial borders and the non-corporeal nature of the activities carried out there.[18] Cyberspace is therefore awarded de facto status as a global space beyond traditional legal sovereignty. These authors present a fait accompli in the form of a normative argument that states should respect 'an emergent cyberspace sovereignty', backed by claims that some states already do.[19] There are no signs that any state is even beginning to recognise the independent legal sovereignty of cyberspace. In fact, the opposite is true: there has never been a time in which states have been less likely to cede authority over cyberspace, however futile or misguided may be their attempts to translate their own territorial sovereignties into the domain. It may be that, in time, portions of cyberspace are deliberately – rather than fortuitously – left relatively unregulated by states with whose jurisdictions these parts are roughly identifiable, but the likelihood of cyberspace in whole or in part being granted international legal sovereignty is very slight indeed.[20] In other words, no compromise is likely to be made to allow for the recognition of cyberspace as a legal sovereign entity, particularly as cyberspace is not an autonomous or unitary actor, nor capable of being represented by a single voice.

Westphalian sovereignty and cyberspace

Westphalian sovereignty is predicated on the basis that states are identifiable with particular physical territories within which domestic political authorities are the only legitimate source of institutional organisation and policy. The norm at work is therefore one of non-intervention in the internal affairs of other states. Violations of Westphalian sovereignty occur when external actors induce changes in, or otherwise determine, the structures and conduct of domestic political authority. These need not occur solely through the imposition of will or force but can also occur as a result of voluntary actions, such as invitations extended to external actors to participate in domestic affairs. While the former would also breach international legal sovereignty, the latter would not.[21]

The most obvious example of how cyberspace interacts with Westphalian sovereignty is in the exercise of compulsory cyber-power. Computer network operations against assets located in another country a priori violate Westphalian sovereignty, although the circumstances under which these might occur differ substantially. Cyberspace operations conducted in war breach Westphalian sovereignty in much the same way as any other form of militarised action against another state. Although the origin and organisation of the cyberspace operations against Estonia in 2007 and Georgia in 2008 are disputed, it is widely thought that Russian security services were instrumental in their planning and, perhaps, prosecution.[22] Both events at some level constituted violations of Westphalian sovereignty. Covert computer-network exploitation (or cyberespionage) also violates this form of sovereignty if the targets are located within another state. The Stuxnet worm is another example of the breach of Westphalian sovereignty, in this case possibly by a combined US–Israeli operation against Iranian nuclear technologies.[23] On the other hand, one state could effectively invite another to conduct actions within its borders, such as may occur in transnational counter-cybercrime operations. Although this also violates Westphalian sovereignty, the exception is tolerated and encouraged because it is deemed beneficial to both state parties.

It is important to recognise that violations of Westphalian sovereignty can be positive-sum. It is too easy to cite all sovereignty violations mediated or caused by cyberspace as negative in effect, painting a distorted picture of why breaches of sovereignty occur. Although some actions (such as war or espionage) are inherently deleterious to the interests of one state actor, others serve the interests of both parties and are implemented by means of contracts and conventions in which a degree of Westphalian sovereignty is surrendered in the common interest. The Council of Europe's Convention on Cybercrime of November 2001 is a good example of how states have come together to tackle a transnational problem while voluntarily allowing for changes in internal legal frameworks and an increase in cross-border investigative actions.[24] Although the member states of the EU are generally, albeit differentially, acclimatised to collectively sanctioned breaches of Westphalian sovereignty, it is remarkable that non-member states such as the United States have ratified a convention that violates this form of sovereignty.

This is not to say, however, that all such agreements and invitations necessarily confer equal gains on all participants. Institutional cyber-power, for example, works to ensure that the interests of larger and more influential countries are served better than those of smaller states, although the latter may benefit in other ways from entering into agreements with more powerful allies. It is also not the case that all such mutual ventures are successful. The Convention on Cybercrime has been criticised on various grounds, not least the fact that several countries within whose borders cyber-criminal activity is relatively unrestricted are not signatories.[25] If transnational police intelligence coordination and investigation are to serve as a universal deterrent against cyber-crime, the non-acquiescence of 'problem' states undermines this ambition. Potential threats to Westphalian sovereignty are routinely cited by these states as reasons for not entering into international cyber-crime agreements.[26]

Cyberspace offers another intriguing possibility. In keeping with Krasner's thesis that violations of sovereignty are so commonplace that they cannot be considered exceptional, it is highly likely that breaches of Westphalian sovereignty may be normalised in due course, regardless of any conventions or contractual arrangements regulating the use of computer network operations against second parties. The development of 'active defence systems' virtually ensures that violations of Westphalian sovereignty will be not only tolerated but automated and thereby institutionalised as de facto defence and security policy. These systems are authorised to respond to attacks and compromises of friendly networks with retaliatory actions in the form of data packets against assets that are often located outside one's own borders.[27] The locations of the sources of offensive actions are less important in the first instance than the attempt to neutralise the threat at source. Although geolocative data contribute to the development of intelligence datasets, active defence is non-discriminatory in political terms. As more and more state agencies and institutions deploy active defence systems, the overall level of violations of Westphalian sovereignty increases globally. It is likely that this will become the status quo. In this sense, Westphalian sovereignty becomes almost irrelevant in day-to-day terms, although any one breach could be used as a political stick with which to beat another state, regardless of whether the violation was intentional.

This creates a paradoxical situation in which violations are both the norm and the exception, depending on one's perspective and the political and diplomatic exigencies of the time. For this reason, the United States is currently promoting cyberspace 'rules of the road' among 'like-minded nations', not only as a means of deterrence, but also to signal what is and what is not acceptable between states who agree to follow these rules. This is one way in which states can undertake routine violations of Westphalian sovereignty while reducing the potential for diplomatic misunderstandings and the possible escalation of unintended actions.

Domestic sovereignty and cyberspace

If Westphalian sovereignty concerns the principle of non-intervention in the internal affairs of other states, domestic sovereignty refers to the ways in which those internal affairs are conducted: specifically, how authority is organised within the state, and how effective is the level of control these political structures exert.[28] Cyberspace has greatly affected both domestic authority and control and will continue to do so. These effects are noted in a wide variety of political contexts, from liberal democracies to authoritarian regimes, and the responses of states of such widely varying organisational forms are often less different from one another than might be expected.

In their efforts to regulate the use of cyberspace within their own borders and by their citizens, states have enacted multiple legislation and instituted new structures designed to administer cyberspace and its attendant regulations. In the United Kingdom, the *Cyber Security Strategy* (2009) brought into being the Office of Cyber Security (since renamed the Office of Cyber Security and Information Assurance, OCSIA), initially located in the Cabinet Office, to provide 'strategic leadership across government for cyber-security issues'.[29] One of its tasks is to 'keep the evolving governance of UK cyber issues under review ... to identify and tackle areas where governance arrangements are lacking, insufficient or are struggling to keep pace with the evolving threats in cyberspace'.[30] Although OCSIA has a specific remit for international engagement with key allies and others, particularly on issues of cybercrime and information security, most of its work is domestic in nature, even if the boundaries between internal and external are often blurred due to the transnational nature of cyberspace. OCSIA's role as the chief coordinator of national cyber-security policy makes it the principal tool for developing and extending authority over British citizens, businesses, government departments and agencies, and over the regulation of cyberspace activities affecting UK interests at home and abroad. It interacts with a very wide range of public- and private-sector entities to achieve policy objectives and is an important agent of institutional cyber-power in the UK.

OCSIA is not itself engaged in controlling cyberspace and the activities carried out therein. Functions of control are delegated to the usual organs of state such as the police, security services and military, and to regulatory bodies such as Ofcom, which oversees telecommunications operators. Police authorities are responsible for enforcing the law relating to proscribed activities in cyberspace, such as various forms of cyber-crime. Specialist units within the intelligence services monitor cyberspace activities that pose threats to UK entities and interests, as do elements of the armed forces. New bodies have also been set up, including the Cyber Security Operations Centre (CSOC) at Government Communications Headquarters (GCHQ). CSOC has both defensive and offensive capabilities, though its principal duty is to mitigate foreign threats against critical information infrastructures, particularly government systems and those of key commercial partners. CSOC and other private and public organisations contribute to developing situational awareness of UK cyberspace, as a prerequisite for prevention and response actions aimed at controlling certain aspects of UK cyberspace.

These examples illustrate that the UK, in common with most other states capable of marshalling resources in this area, perceives cyberspace as a source of threats to its domestic sovereignty. There is perhaps no clearer example of this dynamic than in the number of states currently attempting to control their citizens' access to information, on the basis that certain types of 'content' and activities constitute threats to internal order and authority, as well as to established economic practices. The OpenNet Initiative has documented the growing use of Internet 'filtering' techniques, particularly in the Middle East, Asia and former Soviet countries, but also in Europe, Australasia and North America.[31] The techniques and practices of filtering have evolved into three distinct and often co-existing forms of control.[32]

First-generation controls aim to deny users access to specific online resources through the manipulation of Internet traffic at various levels from the individual to the Internet service provider (ISP) and at national gateways such as submarine cable chokepoints. Second-generation controls adopt a multi-faceted legal, normative and technical approach in order to allow states to deny access to information on an 'as-and-when' basis. Four principal mechanisms of second-generation control are identified: forcing operators to register websites with government authorities and using non-compliance as the grounds for compulsorily filtering 'illegal' content; de-registration of websites not in compliance with national guidelines on content acceptability and propriety; use of defamation and slander legislation to deter content creators from publishing material critical of government; and the promotion of national-security concerns as the pretext for blocking specific Internet content and services. Third-generation controls aim not at physical control but at effecting cognitive change through the use of information and propaganda campaigns, supported by surveillance and data-mining that allow states to compete with their citizens in cyberspace.

The list of states implementing these forms of control is a familiar one, and includes authoritarian regimes in the Middle East and Central Asia, as well as China and several Southeast Asian countries. The use of cyberspace to mobilise and organise dissent is well-documented, such as the 'Twitter Revolutions' of the ongoing Arab Awakening, in Iran and Moldova in 2009 and Ukraine's 2004 Orange Revolution.[33] Although the effect of these forms of electronic civil disobedience is almost certainly less dramatic than is often asserted, their efficacy is perhaps less important than the moves made by states to counteract these forms of dissent. Evgeny Morozov argues, for example, that overblown claims are made for the democratising potential of cyberspace whilst authoritarian regimes are at the same time using cyberspace technologies to close off avenues for legitimate political expression.[34] In this sense, Western attempts to promote digital activism in countries like Iran and China may well backfire by pushing those governments still further to repress online activities deemed deleterious to their domestic authority.

What is rarely acknowledged in Western security discourse is that recent moves by democratic governments into these regulatory spaces have much in common with the practices of other states whose control regimes are often the subject of Western opprobrium and condemnation. The perceived role of the Internet in radicalising Western citizens and drawing them towards jihadist terrorism has prompted the implementation of second- and third-generation controls in a number of Western countries.[35] These kind of fears prompted the US and the UK to push successfully for the removal of radical Yemeni cleric Anwar al-Awlaki's sermons from video-sharing site YouTube, in a clear example of ad hoc second-generation control.[36]

In the UK, the Research, Information and Communications Unit (RICU) is charged with advising the UK's domestic partners on tailoring their 'counter-terrorism related communications ... exposing the weaknesses of violent extremist ideologies and brands, and ... supporting credible alternatives to violent extremism using communications'.[37] RICU's activities involve specialists in 'digital media' and their limited available research output indicates their interest in online environments frequented by British Muslims, for example.[38] The activities of RICU form part of a broader UK government communications campaign at the heart of its counter-terrorism strategy, which states that it is 'vital to use the tools of the new communications age to refute the claims made by contemporary terrorism and by that means to reduce the threat to the UK and UK interests overseas'.[39] This strategic communications project is aimed in part at influencing those British citizens who would compromise the UK's domestic sovereignty from within the country itself. These third-generation control mechanisms are augmented by an extensive communications-surveillance capability, which may be enhanced further by the revived Interception Modernisation Programme apparently called for in the *Strategic Defence and Security Review* (2010), which would enable the interception and retention of communications and communications data across multiple platforms.[40] Similar schemes have been implemented or proposed under the rubric of national security in other Western countries.

There are many other examples that could be used to illustrate how both liberal and authoritarian governments are pursuing forms of control over cyberspace in order to mitigate perceived threats against domestic sovereignty. In the West and elsewhere, terrorism is commonly invoked as the justification for doing so. In authoritarian countries with nascent or established political oppositions, cyberspace has proven to be a significant factor in mobilising dissent and activism, and governments have sought to counteract challenges to their domestic authority through increasingly sophisticated methods of control over access to a wide range of tools and content. Attempts to control citizens' activities through the exercise of various forms of power in cyberspace have unsurprisingly, in turn, met with further resistance. Such is the ingenuity and technical acumen of non-state actors that circumvention of technical control measures usually emerges relatively quickly once these techniques are dissected and understood, although some first-generation controls have proven quite persistent and effective. It is also possible for citizens to try to opt out of domestic authority structures. As political scientist Tim Luke observes, anyone 'with secure computer capacity and network connectivity can virtually secede from any material state formation's controls by cybernetically creating closed spaces, impermeable borders, autonomous regions, special currencies, and private rules'.[41] There are rarely any clear winners in the ongoing conflict over information access, however, and states cannot claim victory or be expected to concede defeat in their attempts to shape cyberspace by technical, legal, or normative means in order to preserve domestic sovereignty.

Interdependence sovereignty and cyberspace

The issue of control is central to the fourth form of sovereignty considered here, that of interdependence sovereignty. Interdependence sovereignty is concerned with the regulation of flows of 'goods, persons, pollutants, diseases, and ideas across territorial boundaries', and is the form of sovereignty most commonly invoked when sovereignty is said to be eroded by processes of globalisation.[42] Many of the issues of domestic sovereignty discussed in the previous section are due to or exacerbated by the progressive deterioration of interdependence sovereignty. Global cyberspace has thrived precisely because of the relatively unrestricted flow of information across national boundaries, a situation inimical to the assertion of territorial rights in cyberspace. This is summed up by the famous Internet axiom that 'national borders aren't even speed bumps on the information superhighway'.[43] Although domestic authority is not necessarily affected by depleted interdependence sovereignty, domestic control is often weakened. '[If] a state cannot regulate what passes across its borders, it will not be able to control what happens within them.'[44]

The debate over terrorist use of the Internet is concerned as much with the flow of undesirable ideas and content across national borders as it is with the effects these might have on one's own citizens. The aforementioned focus on videos of the late Anwar al-Awlaki on YouTube is merely a recent iteration of an ongoing concern that the influence of foreign citizens on one's own population is difficult to control in cyberspace.[45] In this case, the UK government requested that content involving an individual of dual US–Yemeni citizenship be removed from the servers of a US video-sharing site (YouTube) owned by a US company (Google) so that it would become inaccessible to UK citizens. Google was successfully pressured by UK and US politicians to begin to take down this material, although there is every likelihood that such videos will continue to be posted to YouTube, not to mention any number of other websites. Although states with a long heritage of freedom of expression have ordinarily been reluctant to control information and ideas, this is not the case with respect to cyberspace. While there is scant evidence that exposure to 'terrorist' media online is a causal factor in people aspiring to become terrorists, there is certainly a correlation between terrorist activity and the viewing and possession of such material.[46] Government responses to this are seemingly informed by the principle that some information is simply too dangerous to be tolerated, regardless of constitutional or legal protections ordinarily afforded political expression. Much of this material does indeed breach laws proscribing, inter alia, racial hatred and incitement to murder, but rather than attempt to prosecute individuals on these terms – a difficult proposition for any number of reasons – the onus has fallen on web companies to filter political material on behalf of governments, in return for the continued ability to do business – a classic form of second-generation control.

The efficacy of such attempts to restore interdependence sovereignty has, thus far, been limited. A paradoxical situation pertains in which governments wish to encourage cyberspace as a driver of economic growth and, from a Western perspective, the spread of democratic norms and ideals, whilst also trying to control those same flows of information for political purposes expressed in terms of national security. Thus we can see the US State Department promising to support and foster global 'Internet freedom' and openness in early 2010, yet a few months later dealing with the WikiLeaks affair, which prompted calls for clampdowns on the availability of information on the Internet and enhanced judicial powers to prosecute those who release information into the public domain.[47] Although global Internet freedom and national security are not logically mutually exclusive, in practical terms they are difficult to reconcile. At present, it is difficult to see how any government can achieve both of these objectives simultaneously, without substantially altering the ways in which cyberspace functions.[48]

The logical endpoint of a situation in which national security concerns outweigh all others is a highly regulated online environment in which national cyberspaces map onto national physical borders and mirror national norms and standards: in effect, a political 'balkanisation' of cyberspace.[49] A slightly different situation could arise through the formation of political-economic blocs of like-minded nations in which interdependence sovereignty is relinquished in favour of asserting pooled sovereignty at the borders of these multinational groupings. The technical means for achieving either is far from straightforward and, as upwards of 90% of the relevant infrastructure is owned by the private sector, could not be achieved without substantial buy-in from IT companies or extensive new legislation and regulation.

The relative success of China's 'Golden Shield' censorship and surveillance project, colloquially referred to as the Great Firewall of China, has been substantially assisted by strict regulation of the Chinese telecommunications sector. The Golden Shield is not watertight, but the normative impact of persistent and pervasive Internet filtering and monitoring is as important as its technical efficacy, although strengthening of the latter will have to continue in order to maintain the former. By installing sophisticated technologies at network gateways, the Chinese government can set the parameters for filtering and blocking certain types of Internet traffic based on their source locations, or proscribed keywords exposed by data-packet inspection. By controlling some aspects of interdependence sovereignty, China hopes to maintain domestic sovereignty threatened by political and cultural ideas and artefacts deemed subversive to its national interests. At the same time, it wishes to enhance and expand its utilisation of cyberspace for economic gain and political influence. In both senses, it is little different from any other state grappling with the challenges of cyberspace, even if the nature and extent of responses differ between states.

Cyberspace affects the ability of governments to exercise domestic sovereignty in as total a sense as they perhaps once could, although they have been very active in reasserting control over information sources in order to restore internal authority. The effect of cyberspace on domestic sovereignty is substantially a function of the tendency of cyberspace to ride rough-shod over governments' control over what passes across their borders. Even though cyberspace is a medium of information exchange, the information it carries is decoded as persuasive ideas and ideologies, and/or converted into capital in the form of goods and services. While the latter are pursued with vigour by states, the former are the object of equally robust attempts at repression. The conflict between control of the desired and control of the dangerous is perhaps the defining characteristic of the contemporary cyberspace policy environment. Ultimately, the only way to ensure an absence of immediate effect by cyberspace on the various forms of sovereignty is to switch off the Internet, as the Egyptian government attempted to do in January 2011.[50] To attempt this is to fail completely in one's otherwise-stated commitments to democratic process and information access. In the Egyptian case too, cyberspace continued to exist elsewhere, and news of the government's actions spread worldwide, arguably further damaging its reputation in the eyes of those unimpressed by its repression of civil unrest.

Westphalian sovereignty is also a casualty of the irrepressible nature of transnational information exchange and of the deliberate targeting by one state of the information assets of another. Attempts to prevent cyber-attacks and cyber-espionage are leading to a situation in which breaches of Westphalian sovereignty are not only commonplace, but also potentially a normal condition of global cyberspace: what has elsewhere been termed, 'cyber new normalcy'.[51] What is also clear is that cyberspace is perhaps the vector par excellence for interventions that compromise Westphalian sovereignty, whether in peacetime or in war. We should not, however, overstate the ability of such actions to generate strategic effect, although they are justifiably a security concern for all governments.

Despite the discernible trends in the operations of cyberspace and its users, state and non-state, to challenge sovereignty in its various forms, in the words of Stephen Krasner, sovereignty 'abides'.[52] In no form of sovereignty is this more evident than in international legal sovereignty, which cyberspace does not affect in any substantive sense. If the legal integrity of states is guaranteed in international law to which all governments accede, the state is likely to persist for a long time yet, despite the changes wrought by cyberspace and other forms of global interaction. This should not be a comfort to governments but rather a warning. It is insufficient for governments to convince themselves that international mutual recognition is justification enough for their continued existence. Instead, governments will be required to ask themselves how they can adapt to an ever-changing international system in which cyberspace is but one important factor.

The state, of course, is not a unitary actor, and in many cases neither are governments. For the purposes of illustrating some basic concepts, the international system has here been treated as one in which unitary state actors vie with one another for influence. This is a simplistic view easily disproven by the voluminous empirical research on the workings of international politics. In this evolving environment of which cyberspace is part, governments have voluntarily surrendered aspects of their sovereignty in order to achieve gains in the national interest. They have generated new organisations and structures that reach across traditional boundaries in order to effect positive outcomes for themselves and for others.[53] Parts of traditional government hierarchies have been networked within and across states in order to assert authority and control, and the mechanisms of global Internet governance and counter-cybercrime are good, if incomplete, examples of how this process is evolving, both in scope and in speed. In these networks may perhaps be found the future of the state: one in which further aspects of sovereignty are relinquished in order to retain authority, control and, importantly for governments and rulers, relevance.

Sovereignty will persist, but its continued relevance may have to rely more on pragmatic reckoning than on relatively blinkered interpretations of national destiny or reactions to security threats wilfully or wrongly perceived as existential. This is a position entirely consistent with grand strategy, and no true strategist should feel threatened by the suggestion that pragmatism wins out over ideology. A state without sovereignty is not a state. Neither is about to disappear, but the coming century will be a crucial one in the evolving relationship between the two.

CHAPTER THREE

Cyberspace and war

Cyberspace is without doubt one of the most thought-provoking terms in public discourse today. Strong claims have been made both for and against its wider impact. On the one hand are those who claim that connectivity 'changes everything', perhaps even the way that humans think, our basic human nature;[1] on the other hand are those who claim that it merely enables us to do things we have always done in somewhat different ways.[2] The derivative term 'cyberwar' is equally evocative. But what does it actually mean for strategists concerned with the balancing of ends, ways and means in conflict today? How useful is it for understanding global trends and the future of warfare?

We can gain some insights into these issues by exploring the strategic context in which the current 'cyberwar' debate is taking place (in particular, the perceived diminishing utility of force); considering the likely shape of military cyber-power with reference to relevant historical developments and inter-war airpower theory; and finally, discussing the difficulty of achieving genuine strategic effect through pure cyber-attack. The challenge here is to chart a course between the millennial and the trivial, recognising the complexities of military cyber-power, as H.G. Wells did those of airpower 100 years ago as a potentially terrible but ultimately limited weapon, 'neither unthinkable nor blessed'.[3]

Popular discourse on cyberwar tends to focus on the vulnerability of the 'physical layer' of cyberspace to cyber-attack and the ways in which this may permit even strong powers to be brought to their knees by weaker ones, perhaps bloodlessly. The Chinese strategists Qiao and Wang, authors of the much-cited future-war text *Unrestricted Warfare*, are particularly impressed by this idea: 'The battlefield is next to you and the enemy is on the network. Only there is no smell of gunpowder or the odour of blood ... One hacker + one modem causes an enemy damage and losses almost equal to those of a war.'[4]

Be this as it may, it behoves us to look at the drivers of change 'in the round' in a strategic context and with an eye to relevant historical precedents, which a narrow focus on technology can obscure. The relevant strategic context is not merely the period since the invention of the microchip; rather it is the more-than-a-century-long period in which, for a mixture of political, economic and technological reasons, the decisiveness of major war has been diminishing.[5] One of Clausewitz's most valuable insights in *On War* was the distinction he drew between war's 'true nature' and its 'character'; while the latter is highly mutable (like a chameleon, as he put it), the former changes very slowly, if at all.[6] It is reasonable to believe that the advent of military cyber-power is altering war's character, but not that its nature is somehow being transformed also. Thucydides wrote that war arises from a complex of fear, honour and self-interest; this is no less true of war amidst the network flows of cyberspace in our day than it was amongst the isles of the Peloponnese 2,500 years ago.[7]

There are many instances in the history of war in which technological change has prompted changes in the conduct of war which we can use to illuminate the concerns of the present. Above all, there is much to be learned about the significance of military cyber-power by viewing it through the prism of the century-long debate over the benefits of airpower (its ideal and actual tactical and operational employment, optimal form of organisation, doctrine in relation to other arms, and putatively independent strategic effectiveness).

War and indecision

'War no longer exists', claimed Rupert Smith in the first lines of his 2005 book *The Utility of Force*. '… War as cognitively known to most non-combatants, war as battle in a field between men and machinery, war as a massive deciding event in a dispute in international affairs; such war no longer exists.'[8] Qiao and Wang would have approved. But neither was the first to make such a claim. The basic thesis of the 'futility of force' is actually at least 100 years old. As Norman Angell put it in *The Great Illusion* in 1911:

> Man … is coming to employ physical force less because accumulated evidence is pushing him more and more to the conclusion that he can accomplish more easily that which he strives for by other means.[9]

The two world wars showed that Angell's faith in the rationality of mankind in the face of war's apparent economic senselessness was misplaced at the time. Nonetheless, the belief in major war's obsolescence has proved extremely persistent. Looking back, the two global conflicts of the twentieth century strike many as the aberration and not the norm.[10] Indeed, Hew Strachan, one of the leading First World War historians and head of Oxford University's Changing Character of Warfare programme, has argued that 'the pole around which our ideas of war cluster should no longer be major war, itself a theoretical construct derived from the Second World War and scarcely encountered in reality since'.[11] Moreover, the development of thermonuclear weapons by the superpowers in the 1950s, and their subsequent proliferation among lesser states, has raised the destructive potential of major war many orders of magnitude beyond that imagined by Angell to be sufficient to dissuade leaders from seeing it as a rational tool of policy. By no means has war gone away. It continues to churn away in various forms all over the world. Rather, it is war as seen in the shaky black-and-white footage of the D-Day landings or the decisive German–Soviet Battle for Berlin which has waned.

Whereas in the past wars could be made to pay (princes could add to their treasuries by conquering the lands and taking the resources of other princes), nowadays the benefits of victory are dubious at best.[12] Indeed, it is not simply that the material gains of victory are not what they used to be. In the past, a major benefit when you won the war was that you got your victorious army back in more or less one piece. Nowadays, on the other hand, we have a situation which former US Defense Secretary Colin Powell archly illustrated by using a version of the 'Pottery Barn' rule: 'you break it, you own it.' He was referring to the potential for US forces to become mired in a long, resource-sapping war that would, in his words, 'take all the oxygen out of the environment'. The British historian Sir Michael Howard put it somewhat differently, arguing that while 'the first essential' in today's wars is as it always has been, 'to target and destroy the armed forces of the enemy', beyond that, 'we must obey a military equivalent of the Hippocratic Oath: do no unnecessary harm'.[13]

How similar in spirit this is to Angell's urging that 'the morality which has been by our necessities developed in the society of individuals must also be applied to the society of nations as that society becomes by virtue of our development more interdependent'.[14] In fact, there is more than a passing resemblance between the first parts of the twentieth and twenty-first centuries. Each has witnessed ferment over the future character of warfare, which was far from resolved by the events of the First World War. Though the widespread pre-war conviction that land wars in the twentieth century would be short was shattered by four years of trench warfare, there was enormous controversy afterwards within the major armed forces of the world over how to organise, train and equip their land and naval forces to account for the technological developments in aviation, communications and armour which had emerged during the war.

Visions of future warfare

Similarly, there is today a raging debate on the likely character of future warfare which revolves around the 'correct' lessons of current conflicts for future ones: in particular, to what extent should armed forces be optimised for counter-insurgency, unconventional warfare or that even more awkward (but useful) term Military Operations Other Than War. On the one hand, 'crusaders' argue that we must adapt to winning the wars we are in, or we are doomed to defeat, wasted lives and money, and a less safe world in which the contagion of 'global insurgency' will thrive in failed and failing states. On the other hand, 'conservatives' argue that Iraq and Afghanistan are aberrations and that adapting our forces for counter-insurgency is a craven bargain, trading a first-class war-fighting army for a second-rate COIN machine.[15] Policymakers in Britain and America both appear to have resolved upon a composite, 'hybrid warfare': a theory largely driven by US Marine Corps analyses which hold that, for example,

the future does not portend a suite of distinct challengers with alternative or different methods but their
convergence into multi-modal or Hybrid Wars ... This
could include states blending high tech capabilities,
like anti-satellite weapons, with terrorism and cyber-
warfare.[16]

In January 2010, in a speech at the International Institute for
Strategic Studies, Britain's then Chief of General Staff, General
Sir David Richards, used very nearly these same terms to
describe his vision of future wars:

Conflict today, especially because so much of it
is effectively fought through the medium of the
Communications Revolution, is principally about and
for People – hearts and minds on a mass scale. This is
much more than just about cyber attack and defence,
albeit this is important...
    State-on-state warfare is happening and will
continue to happen, but some are failing to see how.
These wars are not being fought by a conventional
invasion of uniformed troops, ready to be repulsed by
heavy armour or ships, but through a combination of
economic, cyber and proxy actions.[17]

In respect of his first point, whether knowingly or otherwise,
Richards echoes the conclusions of sociologist Manuel Castells
that de-territorialised insurgency is the paradigmatic conflict
type of the Information Age: 'The conflicts of our time are fought
by networked social actors aiming to reach their constituencies
and target audiences through the decisive switch to multi-
media communications networks.'[18] But, significantly, General
Richards also evoked the early part of the twentieth century

in describing the current strategic and doctrinal predicament, which he characterised as being even *more* expansive and challenging:

> This is not a change that happens once in a generation, it is less frequent than that. And in many ways this one is more fundamental than from horse to tank described by [Basil] Liddell-Hart. While that occupied the minds of generals, the present shift is one that includes our entire society and therefore impacts our whole security infrastructure.[19]

If it seems that we have wandered far from cyberspace, it is not for want of reason. Strategy cannot be applied to the direction and conduct of war if it starts from false premises about the nature of that war. On the whole, though, much of the debate over 'cyberwar' does just that: it conflates activities in cyberspace such as espionage, crime, hacking and breaches of intellectual property, which are to a greater or lesser degree threatening or annoying to society, and elevates them to the level of war, a state which society has traditionally regarded as legally, morally and strategically exceptional. This is problematic in many ways, not least from an analytical perspective, but also as a matter of practice.

Grandiose talk of 'cyberwar' distracts us from the actual strategic context of the day, which is that described by Smith in his own way as 'a world of confrontations and conflicts rather than one of war and peace'.[20] What we face is a condition of continuing hostility among diverse state and non-state actors, conducted largely by non-military means (most importantly propaganda and political agitation), sabotage and propaganda by deed, unparalleled levels of espionage both commercial and political, and crime. All of this is conducted in, through or in combination with cyberspace. In short, talk of 'cyberwar' tends to 'securitise' a problem upon which traditional power instruments in fact have relatively little purchase.[21] The gist is the same from Angell to Smith and Howard: major war, the rawest exercise of national power – power in the Weberian sense – for a variety of reasons, seems to have lost its place as the decisive arbiter of world events. This has vexed and confused strategists, charged as they are with connecting military means with desired political ends. However, this is not the first time that strategists have been vexed in this way.

Airpower redux

'The Web is shifting power in ways that we could never have imagined', claimed a 2010 BBC documentary, *The Virtual Revolution*. 'It's providing us with new allegiances but it is also reinventing warfare.'[22] Similar claims typified the interwar airpower debates in Europe and the United States. Michael Sherry, in his masterful history *The Rise of American Air Power*, describes the 1920s as a golden age of speculation about the airplane in which,

> because prophecy necessarily leaped ahead of technology, it often read like fanciful or bloodless abstractions, as if designed, like science fiction, less to depict future dangers than to express current anxieties.[23]

The parallels with our own era are manifold. One of the most obvious is the language and style used. In 1923 the British strategist J.F.C. Fuller entitled his book on the shape of future wars *The Reformation of War*, a title which reflected his belief in the great transformative effect of new technology on warfare.[24] Also in *The Virtual Revolution*, in the context of explaining packet switching – a fundamental of digital network communication in which blocks of data are transmitted via a connection that is only open for the duration of transmission – it was pointed out that 'the data will always get through'. This phrase brings to mind Stanley Baldwin's famous House of Commons speech in November 1932, in which he warned 'the bomber will always get through'.[25]

The point here is not that packets and bombers are the same, although it is a relevant metaphor in some contexts (for example, the information-security industry speaks of detecting and interdicting 'bad packets'); but rather that both these quotations show a certain resignation: we cannot escape the ramifications of new technologies. One sees this belief too in the hacker slogan 'information wants to be free', which expresses the belief that technological progress is making it difficult, if not impossible, for states and other corporate entities to limit the exchange of information or restrict access to data.

In the context of this discussion of cyberspace and war, however, it is worthwhile noting the explicit equivalency drawn in the 'cyberpunk' sub-genre of science fiction between the damage potential of 'information-bombing' a society and bombing it in the traditional, high-explosive manner. For instance, in Charles Stross's novel *Singularity Sky* a highly technologically advanced 'transhuman' culture subverts a less developed one by bombarding it with high-tech mobile phones which are able to grant the material wishes of their users in return for information. A recurrent theme in the novel is that information and progress are inexorable and inseparable. In the event, the contact between the lesser developed culture and the advanced one utterly devastates the societal status quo of the former.[26]

It is easy to scoff at the musings of science-fiction authors on the future of war; but in fact their extrapolations of the future from existing trends have often been as good as or better than the professionals'. Gibson's *Neuromancer* is a case in point with respect to cyber-power.[27] So too in an earlier era was H.G. Wells' 1908 novel *The War in the Air*, in which he painted an apocalyptic picture of the effects of airpower on a hypothetical war initiated by light German air attacks on the United States which expanded rapidly into an unwinnable, bloody global aerial conflagration. His conclusion, written just five years after the first flight of the Wright brothers at Kitty Hawk, was that aerial warfare would be 'at once enormously destructive and entirely indecisive'.[28] Compare this with the musings of the professional airman and prophet of airpower Billy Mitchell who wrote of it in 1930 that it was, 'a distinct move for the betterment of civilization, because wars will be decided quickly and not drag on for years'.[29] Whose vision was the clearer?

But the similarities between the early airpower theorists and today's cyber-power ones are more than merely semantic. Both, at root, are concerned with restoring decisiveness to war and see in the new technology a potential means of doing so. For the airpower theorists, writing in the shadow of the First World War which had witnessed the world's Great Powers stalemated in a bloody quagmire of their own making, the aircraft's ability to manoeuvre in the third dimension offered the possibility of attacking the enemy in vulnerable areas behind his surface fortifications. In the words of the famous British strategist Basil Liddell-Hart, 'aircraft enable us to jump over the army which shields the enemy government, industry and people, and so strike directly and immediately at the seat of the opposing will and policy'.[30] Airpower prophets expressed the decisiveness of this new form of war in no uncertain terms. Fuller, for example, invited readers of *The Reformation of War* to

> picture, if you can, what the result [of a mass aerial attack] will be: London for several days will be one

vast raving Bedlam ... the enemy will dictate his terms, which will be grasped at like a straw by a drowning man. Thus may a war be fought in forty-eight hours and the losses of the winning side may be actually nil![31]

Also, as with cyber-power theorists today, the certitude of airpower theorists about the puissance of aerial bombing rested as much upon an acute sense of the fragility of modern industrial society as it did upon the inherent strength of bombers carrying high explosives, gas and incendiaries. In the 1920s and 1930s there was profound worry in Europe that the economic achievements in which they had gloried, their industrial power, the material and cultural wealth of their societies, had also made them hopelessly vulnerable to attack on the home front.[32] Consider the language of Liddell-Hart:

A nation's nerve system, no longer covered by the flesh of its troops is now laid bare to attack, and, like the human nerves, the progress of civilization has rendered it far more sensitive than in earlier and more primitive times.[33]

How similar this is to the apprehensions apparent in the *National Strategy to Secure Cyberspace* in 2003:

Our nation's critical infrastructures are composed of [a very long list of assets beginning with 'public and private institutions' and ending with 'postal and shipping']. Cyberspace is their nervous system – the control system of our country.[34]

Moreover, as with airpower then and cyber-power now, a complicating factor is the intertwining of the underpinning technology with other areas of the economy and political and cultural enterprise. The airplane was never merely an instrument of war; it was also a tool of commerce and a fulfilment of the eternal human longing to fly.

As Sherry put it, 'aviation enthusiasts tended to view flight as a "holy cause", and with religious fervour they outlined its potential to democratise, uplift and pacify the nations that touched it'.[35] Almost exactly the same thing can be seen with cyberspace and its constituent technologies, which are also essentially civilian. Nations consider the sophistication of their digital infrastructure to be integral to the advancement of their prosperity; countries are pumping public and private funds into ever increasing the speed and bandwidth of their digital networks, and in some places monitoring and controlling what their citizens decide to do with this communication power. Which country possesses the world's fastest computer matters as much to policymakers now as which country possessed the fastest or longest-range aircraft in the interwar period, and for the same reason. They are thought to be indicative of military potential as well as prestige.

What was true of airpower need not necessarily be true of military cyber-power. It is generally accepted that in the Industrial Age industrial power largely determined military power. Whether the same correlation exists in the Information Age between the dominant mode of production and military power remains to be seen. The key is probably not the mode of power, but rather the object of its exertion: if the object is the overthrow of one's enemy, rendering him powerless to resist, then military cyber-power is a multiplier of physical force, not a substitute for it, because of the special relationship between industrial power and strategic decisiveness. If, alternatively, the object of putative 'cyberwar' is persuasion, then we might posit some special relationship between cyber-power and strategic decisiveness. The American International Relations scholar who coined the concept of 'soft power', Joseph Nye, neatly encapsulates this logic: 'in the Information Age, it's not just whose army wins, but whose story wins'.[36] There is no doubt that such thinking has captured the attention of Western armed forces, to judge from the recent outpouring of new doctrine on 'strategic communications', 'influence' and 'information operations'. The truth, however, is that we do not know because it has not yet been put to the test; moreover, even if (as may well be the case) Nye is correct, how much sense does it make to locate the 'test' in the conceptual framework of war?

For our purposes, however, if there are lessons to be learned for military cyber-power from considering the debate over airpower, perhaps the most germane is that both the threats and the opportunities presented by the new technology have a tendency to be oversold and exaggerated by its 'early adopters'. And hence there is good cause to worry that cyber-power theorists are repeating an old mistake: succumbing to the 'shock of the new' where more cool-headed analysis would urge caution and more reflection on the elements of continuity than those of change. Again, as Sherry observed wryly of early airpower theorists, 'air prophets were not invariably systematic thinkers'.[37] Their exhausting precision about the vulnerabilities of the modern nation-state – what today's cyber literature describes as 'critical national infrastructure' – was matched by an exasperating vagueness about how defeat would follow from their destruction. Even today, as Eliot Cohen, professor of strategy at Johns Hopkins University, has argued, 'air power is an unusually seductive form of military strength, in part because, like modern courtship, it appears to offer gratification without commitment'.[38]

The fundamental characteristics of airpower are said to be: speed – a function of the lack of obstacles in airspace, which makes airpower highly responsive; range – a function of the ubiquity of the atmosphere which means airpower is highly mobile; and, elevation – a function of the depth of the airspace which means airpower possesses a wide perspective on the conflict below. Cyber-power appears to offer similar things, only more so, which perhaps explains why it has been enthusiastically embraced by air forces on both sides of the Atlantic. Moreover, it offers something else which airpower does not: anonymity, a function of the architecture of cyberspace.[39] This attribute is alarming and alluring in equal measure, because it seems to offer some potential for restoring elusive decision; if the identity of an attacker via cyberspace is unknown, then retaliation is difficult, and perhaps, therefore, the escalation of hostilities, which has largely deterred major war since 1945, might not be effective. In short, cyber-power is even more seductive than airpower, in part because it appears to offer gratification without the need of any physical connection (let alone commitment) to other human beings whatsoever.

Cyberwar is not coming

Airpower has never lived up to the dreams of its most enthusiastic advocates. This is not to deny the enormous contribution it has made to modern warfare. Indeed, virtually unchallenged air supremacy has become more or less the *sine qua non* of the Western 'way of war'. This is an undeniable advantage in conventional war, as no one understands better than a commander who has tried to fight while on the wrong end of an airpower asymmetry. As General Erwin Rommel, whose tanks, troops and artillery were mercilessly pummelled by Allied aircraft in the battle for France in 1944, put it:

> Anyone who has to fight, even with the most modern
> weapons, against an enemy in complete command of

the air, fights like a savage against modern European troops, under the same handicaps and with the same chances of success.

It is entirely possible that an army of the twenty-first century that attempts to fight without an umbrella of military cyber-power against an enemy equipped with this capability will suffer as did Rommel's panzers, notwithstanding their tactical acumen, esprit de corps and the sophistication of their other weapons.[40] It is rather the failure to achieve the independent war-winning effects – winning the war in 48 hours with nil casualties on the victorious side, as Fuller imagined – which has failed.

It is unnecessary, however, to recapitulate here the 'great airpower debate' which has been dealt with cogently elsewhere.[41] Rather, what is useful to extract from the debate is that while military cyber-power is likely to be efficacious, it will not be so in itself. Claims, such as that of the 1994 American commission on protecting national infrastructure, that 'this technology is capable of deciding the outcome of geopolitical crises without the firing of a single weapon', ought to be greeted sceptically.[42] Nor should we single out airpower particularly; it is merely a fine example of a more general hope, perfectly encapsulated above, which may be seen in all the armed services to a greater or lesser degree, that despite the lessons of history, advanced technology can overcome the unpredictable and uncertain nature of war. The promise of Network-Centric Warfare, Effects-Based Warfare, and similar derivative concepts of the Revolution in Military Affairs – popular theories of the 1990s – withered in the cruel realities of the wars that followed 11 September 2001.[43] Technology cannot make up for all the weaknesses of strategy; often what it gives with one hand it takes away with the other.[44]

The literature on strategy is far from insensitive to the double-edged nature of information technology. The state of warfare today is a source of anxiety to those who fight, plan and develop policy for it, because it is much more difficult and complex than was anticipated in the heady days after the end of the Cold War, when some believed in a permanent triumph of liberal democracy and market capitalism (and from which point Western military forces would triumph easily and cheaply over less sophisticated enemies).[45] For the major armies of the world, formed by the conventions of the Industrial Age, twenty-first-century conflict seems unfathomably complex.[46] Invocations of 'cyberwar' thus tend to make matters yet more complex. Perhaps the most persistent concern voiced by those who write of 'cyberwar' is the idea that it deepens asymmetries of power between strong states and weaker states, and between all states and some 'super-empowered' non-state actors.[47] As James Adams concluded his 1998 book *The Next World War*, one of the earliest popular treatments on the subject, 'as David proved against Goliath, strength can be beaten. America today looks uncomfortably like Goliath, arrogant in its power, armed to the teeth, ignorant of its weakness.'[48] Adams goes to the heart of the matter: the fear on the part of 'Goliath' states that they are vulnerable to a debilitating attack by a lesser-armed adversary, who certainly could not tackle them on their own terms. Strategists are also alert to the disruptive potential of cyberspace in changing the balance of power between the United States and its 'near-peer' competitors (as well as non-state actors):

> One reason for the imminent and broad-based nature of the cyberspace challenge is the low buy-in cost compared to the vastly more complex and expensive appurtenances of air and space warfare, along

with the growing ability of present and prospective Lilliputian adversaries to generate what one expert called 'catastrophic cascading effects' through asymmetric operations against the American Gulliver.[49]

The idea is undeniably a useful rhetorical device, as is the regular invocation of a looming 'electronic Pearl Harbor'.[50] Adams described a hypothetical 'cyberwar' between China and the United States conducted by what he called 'War by Other Means'. The scenario rested on the now familiar premise that the computers controlling China's industrial, communications and public utilities systems, its 'nervous system', had been infected during installation, by Western manufacturers, with trojans, which effectively turned over their control to the Americans from a distance. In this hypothetical conflict a Chinese fleet was steaming to the Malacca straits in order to assert territorial claims there which the United States wished to prevent by some other means than sinking it. At its climax, once American cyberwarriors hijack control of Chinese hydropower production and communications facilities in order to cause gradual 'catastrophic cascading' effects on their agriculture and industry, the reality dawns on the Chinese leadership:

> The phone in front of the General Secretary rang. The President offered his condolences on the unfolding agricultural crisis in the Yangtze valley, and said if China needed help, the people of the United States stood ready to do what they could.
>
> Mystified, the General Secretary thanked the President, and then hung up. With internal communications dead, he had no idea what the President had been talking about.

Miraculously, phone service between the Yangtze region and Beijing was restored, and the grim news of the breakdown at the dam was relayed to the Politburo.

The General Secretary quickly understood that he was not in as much control of his nation as he had thought. He ordered the Malacca-bound battle group home.[51]

'War by Other Means' in this imagining is almost wholly electronic, bloodless and decisive, one might say the very epitome of Liddell-Hart's 'indirect approach' – or indeed of Sun Tzu's famous aphorism about the acme of military skill being to subdue one's enemy without fighting.[52] Another fictitious scenario, written by Richard Clarke, paints a slightly different picture of a hypothetical 'cyberwar' between the United States and an unknown attacker.

Within a quarter of an hour, 157 major metropolitan areas have been thrown into knots by a nationwide blackout hitting during rush hour. Poison gas clouds are wafting towards Wilmington and Houston. Refineries are burning up oil supplies in several cities. Subways have crashed in New York, Oakland, Washington, and Los Angeles. Freight trains have derailed outside major junctions and marshaling yards on four major railroads. Aircraft are literally falling out of the sky as a result of midair collisions across the country. Pipelines carrying natural gas to the Northeast have exploded, leaving millions in the cold. The financial system has also frozen solid because of terabytes of information at data centres being wiped out. Weather, navigation and communications satellites are spinning out of their orbits into space. And the US military is a series of isolated units struggling to communicate with each other ... In all the wars America has fought, no nation has ever done this kind of damage to our cities. A sophisticated cyber war attack by one of several nation-states could do that today, in fifteen minutes, without a single terrorist or soldier ever appearing in this country.[53]

What are the key differences between the two scenarios? On a number of levels Clarke's vision seems the more plausible. For one thing, it is far from bloodless. Lots of Americans are killed, as indeed one expects many Chinese would be killed if the life-support mechanisms of their economy and society were shut down. Clausewitz, who reckoned those who sought 'some ingenious way to disarm or defeat an enemy without too much bloodshed' to be fantasists, would have approved.[54] For another, whereas in Adams's tale Chinese electronic systems are disrupted by trojans placed in the hardware by Western parts manufacturers, in Clarke's the shoe is on the other foot. This makes much sense given Chinese dominance now in the manufacture of computer hardware and devices specifically; and more generally given that open societies such as the United States have promiscuously networked their systems in ways that make it very difficult to disconnect from the Internet, whereas the 'Great Firewall of China' and other measures taken by China to restrict the physical entry points of the Internet arguably make it more cyber-defensible.[55]

In both scenarios the attack is strategically decisive: the electronic attack actually disarms the target state. As we have seen, many find this plausible; yet experts such as Martin Libicki warn that the possibilities of 'hostile conquest' in cyberspace 'may be less consequential than meets the eye'.[56] Can 'cyberwar' without actual or threatened violence be war? According to Clausewitz, the act of fighting is fundamental to war:

> Combat is the only effective force in war; its aim is to destroy the enemy's forces as a means to a further end. That holds good even if no actual fighting occurs, because the outcome rests on the assumption that if it came to fighting, the enemy would be destroyed. It follows that the destruction of the enemy's force underlies all military actions; all plans are ultimately based on it, resting on it like an arch on its abutment.[57]

Clausewitz was, of course, a creature of his time, which long predated electrical devices, let alone cyberspace. Let us, therefore, allow for purposes of argument that the 'abutment' upon which war plans are based, the destruction of the enemy's forces which he imagined requiring physical battle, could also be achieved digitally. Tactically, in essence, armies need to do some basic things – move, shoot and sustain forces – for which communications provides the means of coordination; it is plausible that cyber-attacks could degrade the coordinative role of communications to the point that the basic combat functions could not be performed adequately. Strategically, given the ever-increasing scale and consequence of cyberspace in daily life, it is not an unreasonable supposition that attacks upon digital systems could be very painful.[58] Even then, however, there remains a problem in accepting its independent strategic effect: to whom does the victim of an anonymous cyber attack make 'cash payment'? As Clarke concludes his scenario, 'in cyber war, we may never even know what hit us'.[59]

Strategically, the problem here is not merely for the victim, in identifying against whom to retaliate, it is equally a problem for the aggressor, who must ask 'how do I impose my will on the target of attack if I disclose neither what that will is nor my identity?' In terms of strategy, Adams's hypothetical conflict is more plausible, because at least in that instance the Chinese president is under no misapprehension about whose thumb he is under and the course of action he must undertake to remove that pressure. This is not to diminish the 'attribution problem' which is quite obviously exploited by hackers and criminals who, according to the USAF doctrine on Cyberspace Operations, constantly 'amaze those in global law enforcement with the speed at which they stay one step ahead in the technology race'.[60] It is to suggest that the attribution problem is really something which pertains primarily to espionage and crime, where goals may be achieved anonymously and much less so to war which, to be a rational tool of policy, ultimately must be clear about what that policy is.

The false allure of 'cyberwar' lies in the notion that it provides a sneaky way to return a decisiveness to major war which, as noted above, it has lacked for many years. But when states use military cyber-power against other states for the purposes of compelling them to do their will, they still have to declare what it is (even if after the event). There is no sneaky way around this fact. If China were to kill several thousand Americans, or vice versa, and profoundly disrupt the lives of many millions of others through cyber-attack in an attempt to bend the rival government to its will, then the prefix cyber- would be superfluous to the requirement of describing the state of relations which would exist between the two countries. 'Cyberwar' as a 'pure play' option for states is unrealistic, because of the expanse and diversity of their interests and capabilities.[61]

It is worth recalling that the seminal 1993 article by Arquilla and Ronfeldt, 'Cyberwar is Coming!', which set off this debate, was essentially tactical in orientation.[62] It was a vision of moving and shooting more adroitly than your opponent through the employment of better information systems. It was about knowledge as power in a very literal and immediate sense. Moreover, the inspiration for their vision of war was not, as might be supposed, the precision technology of the 1991 Gulf War but the brilliant tactics of the world-conquering 13th century Mongol empire. To reiterate, what is of interest here is not the technology per se; rather it is what can be done with that technology. In this case, what cyberspace does is to allow armed forces to move information around in ways that, all things being equal, can deliver it a significant battlefield advantage. Military cyber-power is a real and important complement to other military capabilities. It does not, as airpower did not, obviate those capabilities or change the objective nature of war.

Military cyber-power is not as strategically potent as it has been made out to be. There is good reason to think that, like airpower, it will constitute a vital element of future combined operations; but 'cyberwar' in the sense of a strategically decisive form of interstate warfare is a confusing and pointless distraction. Western governments, perhaps more so in the United Kingdom than the United States, seem to understand this, to judge from the speech by GCHQ head Iain Lobban to the IISS in late 2010, which emphasised the contribution of cybersecurity to economic vitality while mentioning 'cyberwar' not even once.[63] There is a growing suspicion of the cyber threat being over-hyped (by experts and companies with a vested interest in selling services to defeat it) that ought to be heeded because the threats need to be carefully contextualised.[64] Clausewitz put it this way:

> The first, the supreme, the most far-reaching act of judgment that the statesman and commander have to make is to establish by that test the kind of war on which they are embarking; neither mistaking it for,

nor trying to turn it into, something that is alien to its nature. This is the first of all strategic questions and the most comprehensive.[65]

This is good advice. But perhaps the most decisive judgement is to realise that the correct frame of reference for Information Age conflict is not 'pure play' state-on-state 'cyberwar' in which strategic objectives may be met through cyber *coups de main* on their own. The correct frame is 'cyber-skirmish', a more or less constant hum of low-level activity over a wide 'virtual landscape', often conducted by irregular actors, with few or no single engagements of strategic consequence, however weighty in aggregate the stakes may be. And indeed the stakes in aggregate – that is to say in terms of the smooth functioning of the overarching international order – are significant.

CHAPTER FOUR

Cyberspace and dominion

After nuclear deterrence it is hard to point to a more significant priority of Western policymakers and strategists than the security of the 'global commons', which are described as being the maritime, air, space and now cyberspace domains. Together, these constitute the 'connective tissue of the international system'.[1] To quote the 2008 US *National Defense Strategy*:

> For more than sixty years, the United States has secured the global commons for the benefit of all. Global prosperity is contingent on the free flow of ideas, goods, and services … The United States requires freedom of action in the global commons and strategic access to important regions of the world to meet our national security needs.[2]

There is a lot to unpack in the way of disputed assumptions and unstated anxieties from these two simple sentences. For a start, as the American historian and strategist Walter Russell Mead has argued, what is at issue is not merely the last 60 years of American primacy as some isolated period of world history, but rather as many as 400 years of a 'maritime order' dominated by Western naval power above all.[3] For the US, 'command of the commons is analogous to command of the sea'; indeed, it is the source of US hegemony. The scale of its investment in the instruments of power, with which it ensures this command, is breath-taking, as anyone who has ever watched a single aircraft carrier battle group, one of 11 that America now operates, at sail.[4]

Moreover, the words 'for the benefit of all' represent a value judgement, which is by no means universally acknowledged. Quite the contrary, in fact. The West's 'command of the commons' has been reckoned by many outside of the West (and some within it) to perpetuate a distribution of wealth and power which is unjust and self-serving. The world-systems theorist and critic of global capitalism Immanuel Wallerstein put the case for the opposition several decades ago:

> The mark of the modern world is the imagination of its profiteers and the counter-assertiveness of the oppressed. Exploitation and the refusal to accept exploitation as either inevitable or just constitute the continuing antinomy of the modern era, joined together in a dialectic which has far from reached its climax in the twentieth century.[5]

There is concern that cyberspace lends this 'continuing antinomy' explosive new potential. The main issue at stake is not merely military security, as we discussed in the previous chapter. Nor is it simply the cyber threat to economic vibrancy, which is particularly prevalent in British strategic thinking, as may be seen in the 2010 UK *National Security Strategy*, which underlines how the country has staked its fortune on being 'at the heart of many global networks … both a geographical and virtual centre of global activity'.[6] It is, rather, the evolving nature of what Philip Bobbitt described in *The Shield of Achilles*, his landmark work on the relationship of strategy and legal order, as the 'international order' entire. Bobbitt considers that 'we are at a moment in world affairs when the essential ideas that govern statecraft must change ... owing to advances in international telecommunications, rapid computation, and weapons of mass destruction'.[7]

Certain changes in the international order can be traced back and attributed to high-speed digital interconnectivity. In probing these changes, it has been useful to re-examine the concept of dominion, particularly as it relates to seapower. Before the advent of global digital communications, 'the dominion of the sea' was a vital force in the shaping of the international order.[8] Indeed, for 400 years the configuration of the global commons has been such that those who possessed the greatest power in the commons, but especially at sea, have been enabled to exert dominion over those who do not. Cyberspace, by contrast, appears to change the configuration of the commons creating a dense and immersive global 'information environment' in which resistance to dominion is empowered and control in the sense implied in other domains is practically unachievable.

Since the 11 September attacks on the US, the spotlight has shone brightest on 'global insurgents' or 'super-empowered terrorists', who were among the first to exploit the potential of the changed information environment to catapult local and sectarian grievances onto the global arena. They also recognised the vulnerability of the international order and the potential to disrupt it, using the tools of globalisation against itself. It may be that the importance of such groups is already being eclipsed by more broadly based networked social movements employing 'hacktivist' techniques either on their own or in combination with other forms of protest.[9] It is not yet clear how far reaching the effect of this may be on the international order, though as we have seen in the pronouncements of major politicians on the matter, there is considerable apprehension that the effect is large.

We should not be surprised at the anxious and often acrimonious tenor of debate on these matters. It is essentially a debate about politics in the sense that the eminent political scientist Harold Lasswell described it as the process of deciding 'who gets what, when and how'.[10] In other words, it is about property, of which the English jurist William Blackstone once wrote:

> There is nothing which so generally strikes the imagination, and engages the affections of mankind, as the right of property; or that sole and despotic dominion which one man claims and exercises over the external things of the world, in total exclusion of the right of any other individual in the universe.[11]

While it goes too far to describe the West's historic power over the global commons as 'sole and despotic dominion', it is true that the longstanding configuration of the commons has been highly congenial to Western interests.[12] Cyberspace has the potential to alter that configuration because of a key difference between it and the other domains in which asserting supremacy has underpinned the international order to which we have been accustomed.

The death of distance

One of the strategist Julian Corbett's keenest observations was that Britain's former naval supremacy gave it the key advantage of being able to engage in as much or as little *limited* war as it wished. In his words, limited war is only permanently possible to island Powers or between Powers which are separated by sea, and then only when the Power desiring limited war is able to command the sea to such a degree as to be able not only to isolate the distant object, but also render impossible the invasion of his home territory.[13]

This is simply because the sea is vast and naturally hostile to human life: even when you do not intend on any fighting, building ships and sailing them across the oceans is difficult; and if you do intend to fight it is even more challenging and costly. At the height of Britain's empire, small wars could remain small, isolated and asymmetric in a way favourable to the intervening power, because the world was so big, and the obstacles one had to overcome were so great.

Cyberspace, however, causes the 'death of distance'.[14] Certainly, its pioneers had an idea of it as a form of commons, which they sought to embed in its architecture, but a commons with the unusual property, as Tim Berners-Lee put it, of 'anything being potentially connected with anything'.[15] This is a benign, even utopian view in theory; but it has a dark side too. Small wars are difficult to isolate because fluid cyberspace does not act as any sort of obstacle as fluid oceans do. Thus small wars 'spill their banks' and spread out on the network flows of globalisation. As James Mittelman writes,

the same global structures that convey knowledge and other commodities may heighten insecurity and conflict. The Internet, the ease of travel, and financial networks enable the contagion of violence, as with cross-border criminal and terrorist organizations.[16]

Cyberspace reduces the proximity of social actors to zero for certain types of interaction. As a result, it brings a multitude of spatially distant, objectively weak actors into the strategic mix. In short, the main effect of cyberspace on the present international order is subversive: it changes the relative relationship of power among states indirectly; but it is quite dramatically reshaping relations between state and non-state actors in ways that enable the latter to perform acts of 'resistance' in places and on a scale which never before could they have done. It does this because of its unusual properties as a domain.

Neither fish nor fowl nor creeping thing

There is no getting around it: cyberspace is weird. For defence strategists, it is an 'unnatural domain', and there are a number of other problems with fitting it neatly into a three-dimensional conceptual framework. For one thing, being man-made, cyberspace is more mutable than other domains. For a ship's captain, in contrast, such things as weather and currents, reefs, shoals and other obstacles, the tides and so on, are immutable. Dealing with them is the essence of seamanship. But the 'geography' of cyberspace is not so static: it can be turned off with a flick of a switch, or by destruction or compromise of its 'physical' layer; or it can be changed by programming new instructions at the 'syntactic' level. It is a construct, says Martin Libicki, and as such,

> there is little hard-and-fast physics of the sort that dictates what can and cannot be done in, say, outer space. What can and cannot be done in cyberspace need not follow the laws of physics or the laws of man – although violating the latter may have real world repercussions. There is no inherent 'there' there except as mutually agreed.[17]

The last point represents a particularly stark contrast between other domains and cyberspace. Where is it? All other domains possess some form of integument: the sea has the shore; the air has the land; land has the sky; space has the upper edge of the atmosphere. And there are military forces which correspond with each of these places, with which we are all familiar: the army operates in the land domain; the navy operates in the sea domain; the air force operates in the air domain. Particularly powerful or ambitious countries may dispose space forces focused on that domain. Although the sharpness of these divisions owes much to bureaucratic convenience, historical inertia and inter-service rivalry, ultimately they are based on obvious differences in the characteristics of each domain which impose particular modes of operation, basic formations, equipment type and so on. And there are grey areas in which domains overlap and in which are found hybrid formations like marines, or naval aviation, services which constantly live in the shadow of the more 'pure-bred' services with whom they compete for resources, usually unevenly.

But cyberspace overlaps with and intertwines everything. What is the boundary of cyberspace, which exists any place a human being can catch two bars of reception on a 3G phone? Possibly around its 'physical layer': from a strictly military point of view this would be convenient as it would proscribe in the context of a high-speed kinetic campaign a number of distinct physical targets to be destroyed, disrupted or 'tapped' for the purpose of obtaining information advantage over enemy forces; this is more or less the underlying logic of the 'Revolution in Military Affairs' and its derivative concepts. Or is the end possibly around its 'syntactic layer', which would seem to be the principle that underpins the establishment of Cyber Command composed of uniformed hackers and various technical means for penetrating, disrupting and corrupting enemy networks in wartime.

Yet if, as we observed earlier, 'social relations always begin and end outside cyberspace', then the edge – if indeed there is one – is to be found in the cerebral cortex of the human brain, where individual thoughts, perception and sense of consciousness resides. The technology and social theorist Clay Shirky puts it thus: 'The old view of on-line as a separate space, cyberspace apart from the real world ... the whole notion of cyberspace is fading. [Cyberspace is not] an alternative to real life, [it is] part of it.'[18] This fact is not of secondary importance, it is the primordially salient reason why cyberspace is different from other domains in a way which simultaneously sets it apart and makes it inseparable from them. In their seminal work on Information Age warfare, *In Athena's Camp*, John Arquilla and David Ronfeldt drew a vital distinction:

> In our view, the information-age conflict spectrum looks like this: What we term 'cyberwar' will be an ever-more-important entry at the military end, where the language is normally about high-intensity conflict ... 'Netwar' will figure increasingly at the societal end, where the language is normally about low-intensity conflict ... Whereas cyberwar will usually see formal military forces pitted against each other, netwar is more likely to involve nonstate, paramilitary, and other irregular forces.[19]

Where you find cyberspace and what it looks like depend a lot on the reason you are looking for it in the first place. If you are looking from the perspective of a politician concerned with how one's country will make its way in the twenty-first-century world of 'knowledge economies' which thrive on secured intellectual property rights, creative industries, the high-tech sector, well-functioning financial services and safe electronic commerce, then it makes a lot of sense to view cyber-space as the sea and the nation's wealth as traversing it rather like the treasure ships on the Spanish Main of four centuries past. True, cyberspace is not a place in the sense geographers conceive of the global commons as specific tangible 'resource domains outside the jurisdiction of any one state', such as the high seas and deep sea mineral beds, the atmosphere, space and Antarctica.[20] Neither does it meet the legal criteria of a global commons;[21] nor is it free as are the atmosphere and ocean, as it is owned by private citizens, private companies and governments which have built and paid for its material components. Nonetheless, given how integral it has become to wealth creation, it makes practical sense to consider it as part of the commons to which the nation requires secure access and safe passage.

Equally, if one is looking at it from the perspective of a military planner whose country has banked its security on the potential of small forces to decisively defeat larger ones through 'dominant battlespace knowledge', then it makes sense to conceive of cyberspace as a domain, because if you lose there (wherever 'there' is), you lose everywhere else too. Moreover, cyberspace does have characteristics that are different from other domains.[22] Cyberspace has very intangible borders, to which terrain type is entirely irrelevant; but as with other domains it does have a certain distinct strategic character and concept of operations that necessitates specialist troops. The question of whether this necessitates a *separate service* is a thorny one. The organisation of military services depends greatly on national strategic context, global ambition and the overall size of the force. Arguably, necessity has pointed in the direction of a more unitary view of warfare for decades – not merely as a result of the emergence of cyberspace – and that is the context in which the debate over a putative 'cyber service' ought to take place.[23]

For our purposes, however, it is more accurate to speak of a societal 'netwar' than a military 'cyberwar', to use Arquilla and Ronfeldt's distinction. If a discussion of cyberspace as domain or commons takes us no further than 'it's complicated', perhaps we can make more headway by switching the frame of analysis. Again, it may help to take a cue from extant doctrine which defines cyberspace as 'a global domain within the information environment'[24] and ask, what is the information environment?

Global commons, global village

The *Quadrennial Defense Review* defines the information environment as 'the interdependent networks of information technology infrastructures, including the Internet and telecommunication networks', which it is fairer to describe as incomplete, rather than incorrect.[25] Certainly, the infrastructures of the environment are an important part, but they are not really the main concern of the doctrine writers, to judge from the way that they actually use the term 'information environment' as something that is 'manipulated' or 'shaped' by both sides in a conflict not so much of the physical structures of the network (though that may be a part of it) but of the ideas in the minds of the people whom the network touches. The famous American military *Counterinsurgency* field manual, for instance, says,

> The information environment is a critical dimension [of insurgency] and insurgents attempt to shape it to their advantage ... by carrying out activities, such as suicide attacks, that have little military value but ... are executed to attract high-profile media coverage ... and inflate perceptions of insurgent capabilities.[26]

Clearly, then, 'information environment' carries a strong connotation of simply 'what people think' and it is shaped by non-kinetic propaganda as well as kinetic propaganda by deed.[27] It bears a strong resemblance with media scholars Andrew Hoskins and Ben O'Loughlin's concept of a 'media ecology', which they describe as an 'interaction order composed of both what appears in news media and what happens beyond the media text – "out there" in the world'.[28] In light of this, it makes no sense to draw a line around 'information environment' that includes technology and systems on the inside, and ideas and people on the outside, and still pretend to talk about strategy.

A few observers such as Paul Virilio have been so impressed by the convergence of the virtual and the actual in warfare that they speak of the 'information bomb, capable of using the interactivity of information to wreck the peace between nations'.[29] Virilio is provocative and delights in making conclusions which less courageous scholars would not venture. Nonetheless, by the mid-1990s quite a few analysts were beginning to see the growing puissance of information in warfare in rather similar terms.[30] Libicki, who was among the first of them, defined 'information warfare ... [as] the use of information to attack information', which led him to ask 'what does it mean to attack information?'[31] It is worthwhile considering this in depth, from first principles, beginning with the nature of information itself.

There are three basic things which can be done with information: it can be transmitted; it can be stored; and it can be processed for analysis or manipulation. Before literacy, information was transmitted orally, by demonstration or to a small extent by drawing. Communication was 'one-to-one', or at best a few. The range of transmission of complex ideas was no further than the thinker could shout them, and the only means of recording them was in human memory. About 100,000 years ago we learned to record the numbers of things by 'tallying' (for example, a shepherd used knots on a string to record the size of his flock).[32] But it took another 95,000 years before we learned to record both quantity and type of things with logo-graphic writing (initially on tablets of mud inscribed with a pointy reed).[33] The information environment in this era would have been very local and very small; practically every place was an 'island'.

Over the next 6,500 years the importance of writing to gover-nance, science and philosophy, commercial enterprise and war grew enormously. The 'public sphere', however, contin-ued to be dominated by oral communication, perhaps most importantly as delivered from the pulpit. Until the invention of the mechanical printing press in the mid-fifteenth century, only a small elite enjoyed the fruits of written knowledge. The maximum velocity of communication was the speed at which a letter could be carried, although as a result of improvements in navigation and ship-building the range eventually encom-passed the globe. For as long as information was restricted to hand-written texts held in monastic libraries and the castles of the very rich, knowledge tended to be esoteric and fragmen-tary and the public sphere was wrapped very tightly around the church and other privileged sources of authority.

What was really important about mechanical print as opposed to craft script was not, at first, its mass but its relative orderliness and uniformity. Lavishly embellished, hand-writ-ten translations of ancient texts were always one-offs and never identical. A printed book, on the other hand, was always the same and once disseminated could become an authoritative text (that is, the same whether you read it in Rome or Riga). What is important here is that while print tended to have a bridging and unifying effect in science, its impact in socio-politics and religion, by contrast, was divisive and fragmenting, 'making possible pamphlet wars and doctrinal polarisation'.[34] It is no coincidence that scholars such as Eric Hobsbawm dubbed the era which coincided with mass literacy the 'Age of Revolution', because mass ideational conflicts are practically impossible to conduct without mass media. As the public sphere expanded, so too did politics and war to fill it.

People often associate mass communication with radio and television in the early twentieth century; but its advent was 100 years before then. The *Times of London* was already hitting a mass audience in the early nineteenth century. The major significance of electronic media is not the difference in audience size, but the fidelity and immersiveness of transmission. Sound and image-based communications are qualitatively very different than text because they convey a functional facsimile of reality as opposed to a mere description of it. The difference is highly consequential. For one thing, there is a far greater potential for emotional impact; consider the difference between a piece of information such as Beethoven's 'Ode to Joy' conveyed as a written score as opposed to a digital recording of it played on a device. The same basic information produces a completely different subjective experience. Overall, it means that the public sphere both expanded and detached from physically delimited space in a way that allowed it to enter straight into people's homes in a very intimate way. President Roosevelt's radio-broadcasted 'fireside chats' are an early example of this.[35] It is at this point that it becomes meaningful to speak of 'media ecology'.

It is hard to overstate the importance of this in the history of war and much ink has been devoted to the study of it.[36] The counter-insurgency literature is particularly concerned with the effect of media, with one of the standard theories being that when 'big nations lose small wars' it is not because their forces are defeated in the field but because their domestic will becomes exhausted by the perception conveyed to home audiences (whether accurately or inaccurately) by the media that the conflict is 'unwinnable' or 'not worth it'.[37] Similarly, the terrorism literature was for many years reasonably well encapsulated by Brian Jenkins' aphorism 'terrorists want a lot of people watching, not a lot of people dead'.[38] Former British Prime Minister Margaret Thatcher was not wrong to say at the height of the 'Troubles' in Northern Ireland that publicity was the 'oxygen' of terrorism; 'the hijacker and the terrorist thrive on publicity'.[39]

Digitisation has a profound effect on these things. Twenty years ago just a handful of countries could afford colossally expensive secure and instantaneous global communications. Now anyone with a laptop and a network connection can transmit information, whether 'one-to-one' or 'one-to-many', effectively globally and instantaneously in a variety of forms; process information (that is, copy, cross-reference, cross-check, combine or manipulate it) easily and cheaply with standard commercial software; and store information in vast quantities almost indefinitely on cheap, miniature and portable digital devices, or in the 'cloud', independent of any particular device. Viewed in historical perspective, then, we might say that the 'information environment' started off being local and intimate when humans communicated mainly by voice in small kinship groups and remained that way for a long time until, relatively quickly, they learned to communicate in a transmissible and semi-permanent medium. It then, by degrees as physical trans-portation links grew, became global, albeit confined to those were literate and, latterly, those with access to mass-communications media. Since then, it has rapidly become possible for everybody to talk to everybody else, in principle, as much as they would want.

Thus the paradigm changed from 'who can I talk to?' to 'how can I get people to listen?' Attention is the gold of the Information Age; how to get it is the obsession of those who seek power. The effect of this is double-edged. On the one hand, as Shirky writes, people want to do something to make the world a better place. They will help when they are invited to. Access to cheap, flexible tools removes many of the barriers to trying new things.[40]

On the other hand, the 'new media ecology' also brings with it a 'digital age of terror' characterised by an 'economy of liveness', 'a new ecology of images' and 'heightened partial reflexive scrutiny'.[41] Put differently, we are seeing a convergence of key maxims of the study of war and the study of communications, which is driven by changes in the scale and scope of the information environment: Clausewitz tells us '[war is] not merely an act of policy but a true political instrument, a continuation of political intercourse, carried on with other means', that is to say, a form of communication.[42] According to Lasswell, communication is about 'who says what to whom in what channel with what effect';[43] and what is powering their convergence is the transformation of the information environment caused most recently by cyberspace. This is why scholars and statesmen now speak of 'mediatised' wars, or 'wars of ideas', and are so concerned with shaping the 'information environment' of conflict as much as its material actuality.[44]

The problem is laid out very starkly in the UK's *Strategic Defence and Security Review,* which warns of the 'future character of conflict':

> we must expect intense scrutiny of our operations by a more transparent society, informed by the speed and range of modern global communications. Our enemies will continue to attack our physical and electronic lines of communication. And the growth of communications technology will increase our enemies' ability to influence, not only all those on the battlefield, but

also our own society directly. We must therefore win the battle for information, as well as the battle on the ground.[45]

A few people saw this coming. In the 1960s McLuhan discerned the emergence of what he called a 'global village' as a result of the rise of global communications. War in this situation would, he argued, take the form of a 'war of icons', in which the belligerents would seek to defeat their rivals by the erosion of their 'collective countenance' with 'electric persuasion … dunking entire populations in new imagery'.[46] That is to say, war would be waged through ideas, with the most powerfully resonant of these being conveyed in the form of images. What McLuhan saw building in the early 1960s is now self-evident. Today's public sphere combines, for individuals, the intimacy of communications of our cave-dwelling ancestors with a vast digital repository of knowledge larger than (and in the process of absorbing) the greatest physical libraries; to this it adds the ability to communicate globally and instantaneously. This new digital hybrid of the public sphere has become so ubiquitous that it is impossible to escape the network, not even by switching off the computer. In short, cyberspace is not so much a 'global domain within the information environment' as it is the digital embodiment of the global village.

Cyberspace and insurgency

Fourth Generation Warfare (4GW) theorists were among the first to observe the effect of historical developments on insurgent capacity, organisation and concept of operations.[47] According to Hammes, the theory's main contemporary exponent, 4GW 'uses all available networks … to convince the enemy's political decision-makers that their strategic goals are either unachievable or too costly for the perceived benefit'.[48] Two things are significant here. Firstly, the consideration of the way in which the mass media was altering the space in which conflicts occur. Before the growth of the World Wide Web had really gathered a head of steam, 4GW was beginning to describe the power of connectivity to shift the centre of gravity of insurgency from the local to the global. Secondly, 4GW observed a development which has become perhaps the central problem of contemporary counter-terrorism:

> 4GW practitioners are making more and more use of materials made available by the society they are attacking. This allows them to take a very different strategic approach ... [focusing] on offence rather than defence ... [because they have only to] move money and ideas – both of which can be digitised.[49]

The 11 September attacks remain the exemplar of this type of attack, in scale if not sophistication, but there are numerous instances of it both before (such as the bombings of the US Marine barracks in Beirut in 1983, Khobar Towers in Saudi Arabia in 1996, and the American embassies in Tanzania and Kenya in 1998) and afterwards, notably the bombings in Bali (2002), Madrid (2004) and London (2005). The November 2008 fedayeen-style attacks in Mumbai, which killed at least 173 people, wounded more than 300 and shut down a major world city for three days, are a worrisome harbinger of the death, destruction and disruption that can be achieved with a combination of low-cost civilian systems and highly motivated personnel using basic infantry tactics and weapons. To date, no terrorist or insurgent group has combined a physical attack with a simultaneous cyber-attack, for instance to disrupt emergency response systems, although analysts such as Professor Peter Sommer of the London School of Economics have warned that ultimately they will do so – most likely around the London 2012 Olympics.[50] Nor have there been there any known attempts at pure cyber-terror.

But the search for examples of 'pure-play' cyber-terror or cyber-insurgency, as we observed in the previous chapter on cyberwar, misses a larger point. As Seymour Goodman, professor of international relations and computing, put it, 'cyberspace always touches ground somewhere'; the attacks on America and Mumbai, and the bombings in Bali and London, are examples of cyberspace touching the ground.[51] Al-Qaeda's mode of operation, the whole concept of 'global insurgency', makes no sense without the dense web of interconnectivity that is cyberspace. Without it there would be no global forum through which to transmit their narrative of repression and resistance through propaganda of the deed, no secure global communications capability for planning, recruitment and financing of their organisations, and no open-source intelligence and analysis network in the form of the Internet, which is integral to their functioning. To reiterate, cyberspace is like the chimera: what you make of it depends on the way that you are looking at it and why.

'History will not portray Osama bin Laden as a mere terrorist', wrote Bruce Berkowitz. 'Rather, instructors at West Point and Annapolis will cite him as one of the first military commanders to use a new kind of combat organisation in a successful operation.'[52] John Robb, software entrepreneur and freelance strategist, has made a similar argument, that war is being transformed from a predominantly closed and state-centred affair to a more open one in which 'super-empowered' non-state groups can challenge nations and win.[53] Qiao and Wang also dwell on this point in *Unrestricted Warfare*. Their analysis differs only in being more inclusive in its examples of superempowered 'lunatics', from Bin Laden to the financier George Soros, the drug dealer Pablo Escbar, the founder of Japanese cult Aum Shinrikyo, Chizuo Matsumoto, and the hacker Kevin Mitnick.[54]

Aspects of cyberspace such as intangibility, anonymity, ease of communications and digital ubiquity have had the effect of empowering small groups whose long-term aim is to radically change the existing international order. While the tactical opportunities to cause 'systems disruption' are frightening, how it can be harnessed to strategic effect is complex. 'Global insurgency' theory is currently the most prominent means of explanation. The essence of the idea is that the 'War on Terror' ought to be viewed as a struggle with an 'extremely large-scale, transnational, globalised insurgency', which aims to change the international order through an admixture of propaganda of the deed, subversion and open warfare.[55] Al-Qaeda, its key actor, acts in the manner of what Mark Duffield has called a 'non-territorial network enterprise' which works in, through, and out of borderless, distance-killing cyberspace.[56] For global insurgents, everything is harnessed to the propaganda campaign, which in turn depends greatly upon cyberspace:

> The information side of AQ's [Al-Qaeda's] operation is primary; the physical is merely the tool to achieve a propaganda result ... In military terms, for AQ the 'main effort' is information.'[57]

The major significance of cyberspace to insurgency, therefore, lies in the way that it creates a new 'information environment', in which a concept of operations that prioritises the informational over the physical, makes sense. Mackinlay puts it this way:

> The communities which are the heartlands of the insurgent energy, the energy that has attacked our cities and our populations, live and act on a different

plane. They stretch around the world in an archipelago of individuals, cells and communities; they have
no territory, they exist in isolated but interconnected
groups that are horizontally-related rather than verti-
cally ordered, and their shared sense of outrage is
regenerated by the exertions and the visibility of the
campaign. In these wispy, informal patterns, without
territory and without formal command structures
they are not easily touched by the kinetic blows of a
formal military campaign.[58]

This looks superficially very much like an 'emergent phenomenon'.[59] Indeed, Mackinlay stresses how the techniques of an
insurgency naturally reflect the societies from they arise. If
information technology has given rise to a network society,
then the form of insurgent energy which emerges from it will
be equally 'de-territorialised and globally connected'.[60] And
yet, if we consider global insurgency as an emergent phenomenon, how then can we consider it as a strategic phenomenon?
In nature, emergent phenomena are eveywhere, including the
swarming of bees, ant and termite nest-building and slime
moulds; in the social world examples include software design
and the city streetscape. All of these are essentially bottom-up
processes which are interesting because they produce coherent
(often eerily optimal) results without any conscious agency.
Bees and ants do what they are. That is to say, their 'strategy'
is encoded in their DNA. Strategy, as humans conceive it,
however, requires agency by design, because it starts with
some notion of purpose. Of course, there is an iterative element
to the balancing of ends and means: the aim of policy may be
beyond the means available and, therefore, unless more means
are discovered, the ends must be reduced; but the process
begins with someone setting the agenda.

Again, it is the search for a 'pure play' or wholly new cyber variant, in the case of insurgency, which distracts and disorientates. Taken to its logical extreme, the idea of 'leaderless jihad' shares some eye-catching characteristics with emergent phenomena. For instance, having gained initial prominence for his supposed prowess fighting the Soviets in Afghanistan and rising to mythic fame after the 9/11 attacks, Osama bin Laden then went into hiding, from whence he issued the occasional taped harangue. Al-Qaeda, however, did not stop as a result of this, it might be argued, because it transformed into an elusive networked form in which 'self-radicalised' recruits acting in a manner inspired by, rather than directed by, the organisation's leaders in Pakistan, went on plotting and initiating attacks on their own. A world of pure violent meme-emulation such as this would be profoundly unsettled, difficult to secure and probably impossible to govern. In actuality, though, al-Qaeda is more a blend of old and new techniques and organisational form, and as such it is eminently defeatable. It is a strategic actor pursuing a specific strategy of mobilisation or 'cyber levée en masse' which Audrey Kurth Cronin has cogently described:

> al-Qaeda's most potent sources of strength are its powerful image and carefully crafted narrative, assets constructed through widespread, well-developed and sophisticated efforts to build popular support for the cause ... Al-Qaeda is at heart a brilliant propaganda and image machine whose primary purpose has been to convince Muslims that they can defeat the West and in this way solve their problems.[61]

Al-Qaeda operates in the classic manner of all social movements, violent or non-violent, by using narrative framing to diagnose 'the problem' (that is, establish the grievance or cause), to specify a plausible solution to it, and to provide a rationale for support and collective action; but it does so in a way that is highly adapted to the network flows of the Information Age. It is a network made up of multiple nodes with little central coordination beyond a very straightforward unifying narrative which is constantly reiterated and reinforced by words and deeds.[62] The network theorist Bruno Latour explained the need for this constant reinforcement when he showed that networks are not naturally durable; indeed they exist in a constant state of transience and are, therefore, prone to dissolving if they are not routinely 'performed' in order to re-establish the social relations which give them coherence.[63] That is the function of propaganda and propaganda by deed for global insurgency; al-Qaeda 'performs the network' by administering to the over-arching information environment electric jolts in the form of images of death and destruction which constantly reinforce its narrative of rage.

> In a world marked by the rise of mass self-communi-cation, social movements and insurgent politics have the chance to enter the public space from multiple sources. By using both horizontal communication networks and mainstream media to convey their images and messages, they increase their chances of enacting social and political change—even if they start from a subordinate position in institutional power, financial resources, or symbolic legitimacy.[64]

Whether this is a good strategy – in the sense of being likely to achieve the stated grand aim of changing the international order – is a different question. It has a number of inherent weaknesses. Without doubt, cyberspace enables global insur-gency to take amorphous forms which are hard to penetrate, and to conduct spectacular attacks which are hard to defend against. At the same time, the eschatological rhetoric and sheer murderousness of al-Qaeda (more often than not directed against other Muslims) have the effect of denying its narrative a plausible end-state, while alienating it as an organisation from the population which it purports to represent. '[This makes] it increasingly difficult to distinguish jihad from organised crime on the one side and rudderless fanaticism on the other.'[65]

It is undoubtedly true that such entities are hard to touch with a kinetic military campaign; but equally it is hard for them to act in a strategically coherent manner over the long term. Without a leader to articulate the movement's will, let alone enforce it, how can it employ force to compel an enemy to do its will? None of this is to deny the gravity of the risk that such groups pose to liberal democracies. It is simply to observe that network and social movement theory tend to confirm suggestions that al-Qaeda may be steered towards implosion and self-demise. Digital networks certainly have increased the lethal reach of violent non-state actors, but they have also introduced vulnerabilities.

The natural instinct of the defence establishment is to seek command of the new domain. In the context of a kinetic campaign, this is undoubtedly a sensible aspiration. However, the correct frame of reference for conflict in the Information Age is 'cyber-skirmish' not 'cyberwar', in which case command is not a relevant concept. Moreover, gaining 'command of the sea' proved difficult even for the imperial superpowers.[66] Command of cyberspace is an even more distant possibility.

There has always been an 'information environment', just as there have been many attempts to describe and understand it. In the words of sociologist Manuel Castells, it is '… the space of societal, meaningful interaction where ideas and values are formed, conveyed, supported and resisted; space that ultimately becomes a training ground for action and reaction'.[67] Throughout history, the scope of the information environment grew as communication grew more sophisticated, faster and more extensive, until with cyberspace it became effectively instantaneous and global. With each advance in communications, conflict has expanded to fill the new space. Global insurgents have been among the first to move into the new information environment, where they discovered quickly a strategy for mobilising the grievance of a global Muslim diaspora, weaponising the burgeoning identity crises of the second- and third-generation members of this community, and turning the tools of globalisation against itself.

In point of fact, there are many other networked social movements which use some or all of the ways as al-Qaeda – notably resource mobilisation via propaganda and propaganda by deed, 'flattened' hierarchy, decentralisation and self-organisation, all of which depend on networks. Some of these networked movements such as the environmental group Earth Liberation Front use violence, albeit on nowhere near the scale or of the same viciousness as al-Qaeda, though they are similarly intent on destroying Western civilisation, which they regard as inimically hostile and destructive of the Earth's environment.[68] Many others use cyberspace to enhance their ability to organise various forms of protest, which may include direct action (usually street battles and property destruction, but not terrorism). A good example is the anti-capitalist movement/umbrella group 'We are Everywhere' which describes itself as

> the rise of an unprecedented global rebellion – a rebellion which is in constant flux, which swaps ideas and tactics across oceans, shares strategies between cultures and continents, gathers in swarms and dissolves, only to swarm again elsewhere.[69]

The motto of the Internet group Anonymous uses similar language with a more sinister tone: 'We are anonymous. We are legion. We do not forgive. We do not forget.' It is tempting to dismiss such groups, particularly Anonymous (even more so its offshoot 'LulzSec'), which is traditionally what strategic studies has done.[70] Thus very little is known about them. The nature of Anonymous's leadership, for instance, if indeed it has any, is unclear. The credibility of the few who have come forward as leadership figures – such as Barrett Brown, who claims to be its 'senior strategist and propagandist' – is difficult to judge.[71] Nonetheless, governments are beginning to take notice of these groups. Instances such as Anonymous's attack on HBGary demonstrated that they have substantial ability to coerce, for whatever purpose.[72]

There is considerable debate among scholars about the transformative effect of social media on politics. It has real Orwellian potential for massive social control through what technology writer Howard Rheingold has called the 'Always On Pan-Opticon'.[73] It also has obviously become a new and growing factor in revolution. It is interesting too that the United States recognises the inherently subversive potential of the infrastructure and how that may be beneficial to its own strategic aims, as may be seen in the decision to invest in the capability to provide access to wireless Internet in countries where the existing regime has cut off access.[74] Where the pendulum will come to rest between revolution and counter-revolution cannot be predicted; much depends on the way in which the situation in the Middle East develops. Rheingold, however, is surely right in saying that

> the 'killer apps' of tomorrow's mobile infocom industry won't be hardware devices or software programs but social practices. The most far-reaching changes

will come, as they often do, from the kinds of relationships, enterprises, communities and markets that the
infrastructure makes possible.[75]

The reasons why networked social movements other than
al-Qaeda have failed to deeply impress themselves on the
strategic consciousness of states is not because they require
some new technology. The ways and means to exert power, to
compel, or attempt to compel, their enemies to do their will, are
already available. Various techniques ranging from disruption
and sabotage, both real and virtual, to violent physical actions,
have been shown to be operationally effective. The cause of
their latency is political: none has yet attached these ways and
means to a cause compelling enough to mass-mobilise. Thus,
the problem for future war horizon-scanners is not so much
the degree to which they correctly apprehend emerging technology, it is the degree to which they understand the human
motivations behind the usages of that technology.

CONCLUSION

Cyberspace presents something of a paradox in its tendency to foster both great opportunity and significant threat. Whilst it is not yet clear what its long-term societal impacts will be, there is little doubt that cyberspace, principally referred to in terms of the Internet and the World Wide Web, has already engendered substantial change in many different fields of human endeavour. In launching its Future of the Internet Economy initiative in 2008, the Organisation for Economic Co-operation and Development asked, 'can you remember life before the Internet?'[1] For many of its younger users, there was quite literally no life before the Internet. They are growing up in tandem with what the OECD succinctly described as 'this extraordinary technology'. For those who do recall life before the digital electronic expansion of the 1990s, it is difficult to fully comprehend how greatly information technology has enhanced and altered our abilities to communicate with our fellow humans.

Although it would be sensible to note that cyberspace is unevenly distributed – in some places in the world there is very limited supporting infrastructure at best, whereas in others it is to all intents and purpose ubiquitous – the global trend is towards greater connectivity between people and machines, and a deepening synchronicity between the actual and virtual lives of increasing numbers of people. As Internet penetration begins to level out in richer countries, it is in developing countries that Internet uptake continues to expand rapidly, particularly through Internet-enabled mobile telephony. By the end of 2010, nearly two billion people, or over one-quarter of the global population, were estimated to be online.[2] By 2020, it is estimated that 16bn Internet-enabled devices – an average of between one and six devices per person – will be online in an 'Internet of things'.[3]

Cyberspace is growing rapidly and transforming, if not yet superseding, the manner in which we conduct ourselves in business, politics and entertainment, and in affairs of the heart, spirit and intellect. It is also changing the way we fight. The challenge for practitioners, strategic planners and policymakers is to understand the nature and extent of these changes, together with the new opportunities and challenges. Thus it is difficult to recognise and evaluate the emerging threats and opportunities, and to balance investments in a manner which best mitigates the former and enhances the latter. This is not unprecedented, however. Nuclear war was a practical problem from the day in 1949 when the USSR exploded an atomic bomb to match that of the US. It was not until the late 1950s and early 1960s that Bernard Brodie, Albert Wohlstetter, Herman Kahn and the other 'Wizards of Armageddon' began to theorise it as a means of warfare.[4]

The age of uncertainty or a new age of anxiety?

The advent of the Information Age, of which cyberspace is exemplary, is not like the advent of the nuclear age ushered in at Alamogordo, New Mexico, on 16 July 1945. On the occasion of the latter, J. Robert Oppenheimer, the scientific director of the Manhattan Project, was moved to recall the words of the Hindu holy book, the *Bhagavad Gita*, 'I am become Death, the destroyer of worlds.'

By contrast, while also moved to hyperbole by the awesome potential of the thing they had created, the pioneers of cyberspace adopted a more self-consciously positive and socially constructive tone epitomised by the aforementioned 'Declaration of the Independence of Cyberspace'.[5] Many of the originators of the Internet and the Web worked within government circles and posed no direct threat to the status quo; others set themselves up in opposition to government but with libertarian values rather than destructive intent. Now, governments are all too aware of the potential threats posed by cyberspace and popular discourse is alive with talk of them. CNN's February 2010 'Cyber Shockwave', a live televised simulation of a successful cyber attack on the United States, opened with a full-screen shot of the words 'WE WERE WARNED', as if to leave citizens and policymakers alike in no doubt as to the implications of a failure to secure cyberspace.[6] Politicians are possessed of a sense of urgency and alarm about this new environment and what it might mean for the existing international order. On the one hand, they sense that there is an ongoing transformation of human society as a result of technological expansion, which poses a major challenge. On the other hand, they do not yet, in common with most of their citizens, comprehend the nature of the new order and how to adapt to it, although they understand that they must and sense keenly that there is much to lose if they fail. Since cyberspace is a term taken from science fiction, it seems apt to suggest that fiction can offer a basic injunction about how we ought to deal with it. Douglas Adams' classic *Hitchhikers' Guide to the Galaxy* is emblazoned on its front cover in 'large friendly letters' with the words 'DON'T PANIC'. This is excellent advice.

A complicating factor is that the emergence of cyberspace coincides with an historical era in which the West perceives its dominance to be in decline. Moreover, cyberspace is unusual: it clashes with our habitual patterns of the classification of things. It has effects on power which are counterintuitive, from the perspective of power as the ability to coerce, to compel one's enemy to do one's will through physical pressure. In the first instance, it appears to have been empowering of small groups, less because of the way that it allows them to take on resilient organisational forms than in the way that it enables them to pursue a strategy of *levée en masse* which would otherwise be impossible for a distributed, non-territorial entity.[7] It has spurred the evolution of insurgency into a virulent, networked and global form. It also appears to allow states which are, in the eyes of the West, less rule-bound, advantages over others because of their ability to mobilise criminal hackers to state purposes.

John Perry Barlow's barb about 'weary giants' thus strikes very deeply, for this is indeed how the major powers of the Western world feel at the moment, rather closer to *Götterdämmerung* (twilight of the gods) than to the dawn. The foreword to Britain's *National Security Strategy* written by Prime Minister David Cameron captures this feeling. 'We are entering an age of uncertainty', he says – ironically for a conservative, without reference to John Kenneth Galbraith's 1970s television series and book of the same name, which argued for a 'new socialism'.[8] A popular recent book on the 'new world disorder' heralds this as the Age of the Unthinkable.[9] Overall, however, the current debate has a feel which is very reminiscent of Oswald Spengler's *Decline of the West*, written after the First World War in which he lamented: 'the era of individualism, liberalism and democracy, of humanitarianism and freedom, is nearing its end'.[10]

Was Spengler wrong or just premature? It is not for this analysis to say, for surely the answer depends upon many factors other than cyberspace. There is no doubt that the global distribution of power and wealth is shifting, but the reasons for this relate also to deep historical processes, demography, educational levels and scientific creativity, geography and access to natural resources. To be sure, as we discussed in the chapter on cyberspace and dominion, cyberspace does have a direct effect on the information environment; and no doubt cyberspace is highly disruptive of many processes heretofore considered safe, such as the exchange of money and the relative security of personal, industrial and governmental data, as we can see from the burgeoning statistics on cyber-crime and cyber-espionage.

In short, we all live in a densely interconnected information environment which is as rich as any primeval rainforest with delicious things to eat and scary things to be eaten by. We are, however, as a society and as individuals, new to this environment. A few of us have adapted quickly, but the vast majority of us behave as the denuded Adam and Eve after their expulsion from the Garden of Eden, ignorant of and ill-equipped against the new dangers of our expanded world. Many casual users of cyberspace are still possessed of an innocence that makes them an easy target for predatory criminals, identity fraudsters and con artists. To secure itself, the network society needs to mature and to 'cover up', which it seems to be at least in the process of doing. As Libicki puts it, 'today's security problems, may, in retrospect, [have] come to be understood as the shakedown process of taking a silicon creature from a cosseted, closed institutional environment and opening it to the real world'.[11]

If cyberspace is not quite the hoped-for Garden of Eden, it is also not quite the pestilential swamp of the imagination of the cyber-alarmists. Indeed, from the perspective of the West (which may or may not be in decline for other reasons) it is really very advantageous. A question we have asked ourselves throughout this research is whose problems would we rather have with respect to cyberspace, those of the West or those who oppose and fear it? In October 1945, George Orwell wrote a short essay entitled 'You and the Atom Bomb' in which he claimed:

> I think the following rule would be found gener-
> ally true: that ages in which the dominant weapon is
> expensive or difficult to make will tend to be ages of
> despotism, whereas when the dominant weapon is
> cheap and simple, the common people have a chance.
> Thus, for example, tanks, battleships and bombing
> planes are inherently tyrannical weapons, while rifles,
> muskets, long-bows and hand-grenades are inher-
> ently democratic weapons. A complex weapon makes
> the strong stronger, while a simple weapon – so long
> as there is no answer to it – gives claws to the weak.[12]

This should be heartening, because cyberspace is both complex *and* simple. Recent events suggest that weaponising cyberspace is in fact very challenging because of this complexity. To be sure, the physical instruments of a cyber-attack are extremely cheap. The Stuxnet virus may have accomplished relatively cleanly what a large air force might have struggled to do messily but, rightly, much attention has been paid to the virus's remarkable sophistication. A large amount of very high-grade intelligence about its intended target was required in order for it to work. This was not, according to experts who have analysed it, the work of hackers alone:

> It had to be the work of someone who knew his way
> around the specific quirks of the Siemens controllers

and had an intimate understanding of exactly how the Iranians had designed their enrichment operations. In fact, the Americans and the Israelis had a pretty good idea.[13]

And even then, the longevity of its effects on Iranian enrichment capabilities are questionable. As with all other weapons systems (with the exception of the hydrogen bomb, arguably) it required the combination of significant other resources in order to achieve strategic effect. In hindsight, we may look at it as the Zeppelin bomber of its day: expensive and complex to operate, a foreshadow of yet more expense and complexity. In short, far from demonstrating a smoothing of the existing asymmetry of power, it actually shows a reinforcement of that asymmetry: cyber-power rewards already powerful states with even more capability and, when push comes to shove, it would appear that Western powers have thought hard about cyber-attack and are pretty good at it.

Again, a comparison to airpower is apt. Certainly, virtually unchallenged air supremacy and air–ground coordination has become more or less the *sine qua non* of the Western 'way of war', or what in his book *Military Power* Stephen Biddle described as the 'modern system' of warfare.[14] The advent of the 'modern system' caused a bifurcation of military power between armies that 'got it' and armies that did not, with the latter being soundly thrashed by the former even when they possessed the same, or similar, weapons and numerical superiority. A similar scenario is likely with respect to cyber-power. Armies which are able to defend their networks will accrue distinct advantages from 'network-enabling' them, while armies that do not possess such ability will not enjoy any such advantage, and they will be punished harshly for trying to 'network-enable' practically anything.

In other ways, however, cyberspace really does give 'claws to the weak'. It would be absurd to deny that the West's historic power has depended for many centuries upon mastery of the dominant weapon systems of the day. There is a rare unity among historians on the basic point that Europeans about four centuries ago began to emphatically outstrip the other peoples of the earth largely because, in the words of William H. McNeill, of a 'self-reinforcing cycle in which [their] military organisation sustained, and was sustained by, economic and political expansion'.[15] They were, in other words, better at war than everyone else, which made them richer and hence more deadly still, and as a result they were able to 'set the rules'. However, the West has serially failed to exert dominion through the power of its weapons since the era of decolonisation. Its occasional attempts to do so, in Vietnam, Iraq and Afghanistan, have proved costly débacles which foundered on the basic problem that the West has lost the urge to translate its superiority of arms into direct rule of other people against their will. Instead, it attempts to exert dominion through the power of its ideas which, by and large, it still does. Though undoubtedly they would balk at being characterised as a 'dominant weapon system' or as any kind of weapon system full stop, the truth is that illiberal regimes now perceive cyberspace entities such as Facebook, Google and Twitter as daggers pointed at their throats, or at least as swords hanging over their heads. Western governments have been very slow to recognise, at least publicly, this fact. Their opponents, on the other hand, have demonstrated over and over that they fear much more the West as an irresistible and insensate force of cultural contamination and ideational infiltration, which is why traditional Islamic societies worry more about Britney Spears and Barbie dolls than they do Joint Direct Attack Munitions and *Tomahawks*.[16]

Softly, softly catchee monkey...

In medicine, 'watchful waiting' is an approach to complex problems in which time is permitted to pass while the patient is observed and before any intervention or therapy is attempted. The logic of it is twofold. Firstly, the problem may solve itself without any intervention. Secondly, intervening before the problem is understood runs the risk of making it worse. The term 'masterly inactivity' has approximately the same meaning and a long and respectable history in politics and strategy. A degree of it in the context of cyberspace would not be out of place.

To be sure, the state needs to adapt, to be 'rediscovered' as the American philosopher Jon Dewey writing in the 1920s put it. If they do not adapt because of outmoded 'belief in political fixity [and] the sanctity of some form of state concentrated by the efforts of our fathers and hallowed by tradition', this will be 'an invitation to revolt and revolution'.[17] This is perhaps one reason why governments relying on traditional forms of repression and control are having so many problems within their own sovereign borders when those problems are 'caused' or mediated by cyberspace. Despite the perceived problems of transnational radicalisation and terrorism in the West, this remains an issue which Western governments would rather have than the internal political problems of, say, Iran or China, countries with strong, politically motivated regimes of cyberspace control. Their domestic sovereignty is threatened by cyberspace in a manner in which Western governments are not, despite rhetoric to the contrary. There is perhaps much to be wary of, therefore, in current attempts by Western liberal governments to translate old models of authority and control into cyberspace, given that such attempts elsewhere have delivered a decidedly mixed bag of results.

Dewey also observed that maintaining and managing statehood is always an 'experimental process', which is sometimes characterised by 'diverse degrees of blindness and accident, and... unregulated procedures of cut and try, of fumbling and groping'. Moreover, he noted, 'conditions and action of inquiry and knowledge are always changing', in which case, 'the state must always be rediscovered'.[18] In a sense, the state is subject to adaptive pressures rather as business, in Schumpeter's terms, is subject to 'creative destruction ... mutation that incessantly revolutionises the economic structure from within, incessantly destroying the old one, incessantly creating a new one'.[19] Perhaps then we should take a lesson from the business pages, which for years were replete with stories of the leviathan hierarchical institutions being outmanoeuvred by their smaller and nimbler competitors. That the volume of such stories has slowed considerably suggests that businesses have already adapted to succeed in the new environment. Many of today's business leviathans, even in the information-technology sector, predated the Internet; and the nimblest and most successful dot-com start-ups have all acquired substantial 'bricks and mortar' hierarchies as they have grown, buying physical capital such as business headquarters and technological hardware.

In short, states can adapt. Open, democratic, law- and norm-governed countries are in a better position to do so than are closed and undemocratic ones. This is perhaps a surprising conclusion given the tone of the extant debate, driven as it is by interest-driven alarmism and tinged by the parallel narrative of sustained Western decline. Nonetheless, it is true when time is taken to consider the matter 'in the round' and in historical perspective. It is argued, for instance, that small and medium states may benefit greatly by employing 'cyber-mercenaries' to do their dirty work. The danger of this happening is not to be scoffed at, particularly as we have already seen signs of it, as noted earlier of the cyberspace dimension of Russia's conflicts with Estonia and Georgia. According to Richard Clarke, this could make cyber-war 'the next great leveller'. He goes on:

> Given a handful of extremely talented hackers, a relatively effective intelligence agency, and a pot of funds to hire cyber mercenaries and insiders, many nations could compensate for their smaller size by letting an army of computers go to war for them.[20]

There is good reason to doubt this, not only because cyber-attacks such as those on Estonia and Georgia have been less impressive than has been claimed, but because over many centuries now it has been clear to modern nation-states that their interests and that of private military enterprise are, in the long run, incompatible.[21] Weak states have often turned to piracy or privateers for their military needs in the past, usually with poor results because mercenaries are wont to put their own interest before that of their clients, who nonetheless may be left to pay the consequences of the actions of their soldiers of fortune.

One major effect of cyberspace is that it makes it easier to subvert and harder to govern. This has certainly caused the West substantial bedevilment in its efforts to defeat complex insurgencies in Iraq and Afghanistan, as well as to meet the challenge of global insurgency. Yet, though the avowed strategy of al-Qaeda is to topple the repressive secular regimes of the Middle East and replace them with repressive Islamic ones, none of the recent 'Twitter revolutions' there have been led or inspired by Islamist ideology. On the contrary, these revolutions have rung to cries for real democratic representation, fundamental human rights and an end to decades of stultifying corruption. The West's ideals, it bears emphasising, however often enslaved to realpolitik, are deeply subversive and far more in accordance with the postulated and actual ideals of cyberspace. One senses this recognition in UK Foreign Secretary William Hague's speech to the 2011 Munich Security Conference, in which he stated,

> as liberal democracies we also have a compelling vision in supporting democratic ideals in cyberspace, and working to convince others of this vision. When we talk about defending ourselves against cyber threats, we also mean the threat against individual rights to freedom of expression that is posed by states blocking Internet communications. The free flow of ideas and information is an essential underpinning of liberty.[22]

This is all the more clever and powerful for being true. The most powerful Middle Eastern martyr at the time of writing has been Mohamed Bouazizi, a Tunisian street vendor who set himself alight on 17 December 2010 in protest at the confiscation of his wares and the serial infliction of humiliation upon him by agents of the government. His death sparked a wave of revolt throughout the region which has thus far toppled from power Zine el Abidine Ben Ali in Tunisia, Hosni Mubarak in Egypt and Muammar Gadhafi in Libya, and threatens other autocrats still. By contrast, Osama bin Laden's death at the hands of American Navy SEALs in a compound in Pakistan was greeted even within the Muslim world with a sense of muted relief.

Finally, a last general effect of cyberspace is that it makes data easier to steal and harder to conceal. The recent WikiLeaks affair is illustrative of this development. Of all the challenges to the workings of democratic states, this is the most significant and revealing of the vast gulf between where states need to be with respect to data security, and where they actually are now. The key figure here, though, is not WikiLeaks head Julian Assange, nor even Private Bradley Manning, the US intelligence analyst who has been imprisoned in the US for allegedly passing on the US Embassy cables to the website. Bruce Sterling hits the nail on the head when he notes that the problem basically amounted to naivety:

> It did not occur to [Manning's] superiors that a bored soldier in a poorly secured computer system would download hundreds of thousands of diplomatic cables. Because, well, why? They're very boring. Soldiers never read them. The malefactor has no use for them. They're not particularly secret. They've got nothing much to do with his war. He knows his way around the machinery, but Bradley Manning is not any kind of black hat programming genius.[23]

Well-known terrorism specialist Marc Sageman's theory of 'leaderless jihad' holds that, at root, the terrorist threat is posed by 'bunches of guys … lost men [who] would congregate at mosques and find others like them[selves]'.[24] With Manning, however, we do not even have a bunch of guys. There is one bored, resentful man who 'just discovered some awesome capacities in his system that his bosses never knew it had'.[25] Which brings particular force to a point made frequently by Libicki, possibly the last word that need be said on defence in cyberspace for some time:

> There is no forced entry in cyberspace. If a destructive message gets into a system, it must be entirely across pathways that permit such a message to get through. Some pathways are deliberate design choices and have

been inadequately guarded. Some arise from defects in the software. Some may be put there by attackers themselves after they have found the first pathway – but that pathway must pre-exist one way or another.[26]

Closing these gaps is undoubtedly a lengthy challenge. That said, even here the challenge is greater for repressive states than it is for liberal and transparent ones. Transparency is awkward for democracies; it is anathema to autocracies.

Although there are structural tensions between the forces of globalisation and state sovereignty, states can remain relevant actors by becoming 'network states': 'nation-states, despite their multidimensional crises, do not disappear; they transform themselves to adapt to the new context'.[27] They form networks amongst themselves to share sovereignty; they support and sponsor international institutions and supranational organisations to tackle global issues; they devolve authority to local governance structures and intergovernmental networks.[28] As it adapts to the new reality, the West has begun to cotton on to the fact that the dominant mode of thinking that has often characterised strategy – that power comes from the barrel of a gun – is no longer quite as true as it was. Security, of course, still depends to a degree upon the potency of our arms, but they are not the single most important factor.

We would suggest, rather, that Castells's argument that states will not bring about 'a system of constitutionally founded, networked, global governance' on their own is correct. It will be 'global civil society acting on the public mind' via communications networks that will overcome 'historical inertia' and cause states 'to accept the reality of their limited power in exchange for increasing their legitimacy and efficiency'.[29] The claims of global protest movements such as We Are Everywhere (described in this particular case as 'an unprecedented global rebellion') are occasionally overblown, but perhaps there is a kernel of truth to them for which we might be grateful. The networks of global communication are integral to the reformation of global politics, as they have always been to its formation. It is the duty of strategists to the people they serve to recognise that reformation is not the enemy, but the very substance of politics. Strategists have an opportunity to address the benefits of cyberspace as much as its threats. Cyberspace has its myriad problems, but a true strategic sensibility demands that long-term interests prevail over short-term opportunism. To fail on this score is to reduce cyberspace to a bit-part in a zero-sum game, the likes of which plagued the world during the Cold War. A return to a winner-takes-all modality is neither desirable nor necessary, despite the substantial challenges cyberspace presents. A grand strategic vision of cyberspace can assist states in navigating the informational turbulence in which contemporary international politics appears to find itself. They will be required to rediscover themselves and, hopefully, to rediscover how to communicate with others. Cyberspace is potentially a key component of a positive-sum politics: surely the purest strategy there is.

NOTES

Introduction

1   *A Strong Britain in an Age of Uncertainty: The National Security Strategy* (London: The Stationery Office, 2010), p. 3.

2   The network society is formally defined by Manuel Castells in *Communication Power* (Oxford: Oxford University Press, 2009), p. 24.

3   The White House, *National Security Strategy* (2010), p. 27.

4   Anna Mulrine, 'CIA Chief Leon Panetta: The Next Pearl Harbor Could be a Cyberattack', *Christian Science Monitor*, 9 June 2011, http://www.csmonitor.com/USA/Military/2011/0609/CIA-chief-Leon-Panetta-The-next-Pearl-Harbor-could-be-a-cyberattack.

5   Bruce Sterling, *The Hacker Crackdown* (New York: Bantam, 1994), p. 19.

6   Canadian Broadcasting Corporation, 'Marshall McLuhan in Conversation with Norman Mailer', The Way It Is, broadcast 26 November 1967.

7   John Perry Barlow, *Crime and Puzzlement* (June 1990), http://w2.eff.org/Misc/Publications/John_Perry_Barlow/HTML/crime_and_puzzlement_1.html.

8   The Electronic Numerical Integrator and Computer (ENIAC), built by a team at the University of Pennsylvania, used vacuum-tube technology to make calculations up to 1,000 times faster than the electro-mechanical machines it replaced.

9   Gordon E. Moore, 'Cramming More Components onto Integrated Circuits', *Electronics*, vol. 38, no. 8, April 1965, ftp://download.intel.com/museum/Moores_Law/Articles-press_Releases/Gordon_Moore_1965_Article.pdf.

10 Equivalent to one thousand billion gigabytes. One byte is, generally speaking, equivalent to one character of text.

11 CISCO Visual Networking Index 2011, http://www.cisco.com/en/US/solutions/collateral/ns341/ns525/ns537/ns705/ns827/white_paper_c11-481360.pdf.

12 Mark Ward, 'A Brief History of Hacking', BBC News, 9 June 2011, http://www.bbc.co.uk/news/technology-13686141.

13 Steven Levy, *Hackers: Heroes of the Revolution* (New York: Dell, 1984), pp. 18–19.

14 Levy, p. 25.

15 *Ibid.*, p. 32.

16 *Ibid.*, pp. 32–3.

17 Fred Turner, *From Counterculture to Cyberculture* (Chicago, IL: University of Chicago Press, 2006).

18 Stewart Brand, *The Media Lab: Inventing the Future at MIT* (New York: Penguin, 1987), p. 202.

19 Even today, long after fibre-optic systems made phone hacking by manipulation of tones obsolete, the major hacking magazine is still titled *2600: The Hacker Quarterly*. See http://www.2600.com/.

20 Sterling, p. 36.

21 See Scott Brown, 'WarGames: A Look Back at the Film that Turned Phreaks and Geeks into Stars', *Wired*, 21 July 2008, http://www.webcitation.org/5v9xgcyHQ.

22 Patrick S. Ryan, 'War, Peace, or Stalemate: Wargames, Wardialing, Wardriving and the Emerging Market for Hacker Ethics', *Virginia Journal of Law and Technology*, vol. 9, no. 7, Summer 2004, p. 9.

23 Quoted in Brown.

24 Katie Hafner, *Where Wizards Stay Up Late: The Origins of The Internet* (New York: Simon & Schuster, 1998).

25 Jamie Murphy et al., 'Computers: The 414 Gang Strikes Again', *Time*, 29 August 1983, http://www.time.com/time/magazine/article/0,9171,949797,00.html.

26 See Thomas Rid, 'Cyberwar will not Take Place', *Journal of Strategic Studies* (forthcoming, 2011), http://www.tandfonline.com/doi/abs/10.1080/01402390.2011.608939.

27 Dorothy E. Denning, *Information Warfare and Security* (Boston, MA: Addison-Wesley, 1999), pp. 5–6.

28 A good example is Alan D. Campen et al (eds.), *Cyberwar: Security, Strategy and Conflict in the Information Age* (Fairfax, VA: AFCEA Press, 1996).

29 Suelette Dreyfus and Julian Assange, *Underground: Hacking, madness and obsession on the electronic frontier* (Kew, Australia: Reed Books, 1997), p. 12.

30 *Inside WikiLeaks* (London: Jonathan Cape, 2011) by Assange's number two Daniel Domscheit-Berg provides a most illuminating account.

31 Quoted in Denning, p. 45.

32 For an account of the WANK-worm's attack on NASA see Dreyfus and Assange, chap. 1. As with cyberspace, the concept of a computer worm originated in science fiction. John Brunner's novel *The Shockwave Rider* (London: Harper and Row, 1975) describes the creation by a rebel programmer of a 'tapeworm', which is released into the all-powerful computer network of a repressive regime. Ultimately, in a bid to destroy the worm the regime has to switch off the network, in the process destroying its means of societal control.

33 David Leigh and Luke Harding speculate on these lines in *WikiLeaks: Inside Julian Assange's War on Secrecy* (London: Guardian Books, 2011). p. 42.

34 Domscheit-Berg, p. 15.

35 Dreyfus and Assange, p. 34.

36 The exploits of Cap'n Crunch and other phone phreakers are described in Ron Rosenbaum, 'Secrets of the Little Blue Box', *Esquire*, October 1971, pp. 117–25 and 222–6.

37 Quoted in Rosenbaum, p. 120.

38 The following categories are derived from Roger Grimes, 'Your Guide to the Seven Types of Malicious Hackers', InfoWorld, 8 February 2011, http://www.infoworld.com/d/security-central/your-guide-the-seven-types-malicious-hackers-

636?source=IFWNLE_nlt_sec_2011-02-08.

39 See Dreyfus and Assange, pp. 59–62.

40 Quoted in Ward, 'A Brief History of Hacking'.

41 See Robert Lemos, 'Stuxnet Attack More Effective than Bombs', InfoWorld, 19 January 2011, http://www.infoworld.com/t/malware/stuxnet-attack-more-effective-bombs-888.

42 Richard Clarke, 'China's Cyberassault on America', Wall Street Journal, 15 June 2011.

43 Quoted in Dawn S. Onley and Patience Walt, 'Red Storm Rising', Government Computer News, 17 August 2006, http://gcn.com/Articles/2006/08/17/Red-storm-rising.aspx?Page=1.

44 Quoted in Kim Zelter, 'Google to Stop Censoring Search Results in China After Hack Attack', Wired, 12 January 2010, http://www.wired.com/threatlevel/2010/01/google-censorship-china/.

45 Ron Deibert and Rafal Rohozinski, Tracking GhostNet: Investigating a Cyber Espionage Network, Information Warfare Monitor report JR02-2009, 29 March 2009, http://www.infowar-monitor.net/ghostnet.

46 Ibid., p. 48.

47 Ibid., p. 48.

48 Quoted in Joshua Davis, 'Hackers Take Down the Most Wired Country in Europe', Wired, 21 August 2007, http://www.wired.com/politics/security/magazine/15-09/ff_estonia.

49 Mark Landler and John Markoff, 'Digital Fears After Data Siege in Estonia', New York Times, 29 May 2007, http://www.nytimes.com/2007/05/29/technology/29estonia.html.

50 Quoted in Davis.

51 See Dancho Danchev, 'Coordinated Russia vs Georgia Cyberattack in Progress', ZDNet, 11 August 2008, http://www.zdnet.com/blog/security/coordinated-russia-vs-georgia-cyber-attack-in-progress/1670; also John Markoff, 'Before the Gunfire: Cyberattacks', New York Times, 12 August 2008, http://www.nytimes.com/2008/08/13/technology/13cyber.html.

52 Richard A. Clarke, Cyberwar: The Next Threat to National Security and What to do About It (New York: Harper Collins, 2010), pp. 30–1.

53 James A. Lewis, The 'Korean' Cyberattacks and their Implications for Cyber Conflict (Washington DC: Center for Strategic and International Studies, October 2009), http://csis.org/files/publication/091023_Korean_Cyber_Attacks_and_Their_Implications_for_Cyber_Conflict.pdf.

54 See the BBC World Service documentary, 'The PR Battle for the Caucasus', broadcast 3 November 2008, http://www.bbc.co.uk/worldservice/documentaries/2008/10/081029_caucases_doc.shtml.

55 Clarke, p. 21.

56 See GreyLogic, Project Grey Goose, Phase II Report: 'The Evolving State of Cyber Warfare' (March 2009), http://www.fserror.com/pdf/GreyGoose2.pdf.

57 Enekin Tikk et al, Cyberattacks Against Georgia: Legal Lessons Identified (Tallinn: Cooperative Cyber Defence Centre of Excellence, 2008), http://www.carlisle.army.mil/DIME/documents/Georgia%201%200.pdf.

58 See Matthew C. Waxman, 'Cyberattacks and the Use of Force: Back to the Future of Article 2(4)', Yale Journal of International Law, vol. 36, no. 2, 2010, p. 458.

59 Michael Evans, 'From Kadesh to Kandahar', Naval War College Review,

vol. 56, no. 3, Summer 2003, pp. 133–4.

60 Brian Boyd, 'Robin Hood of Hacking', *Irish Times*, 6 June 2010, http://www.irishtimes.com/newspaper/weekend/2010/0626/1224273343835.html.

61 Jaron Lanier, *You are not a Gadget* (London: Penguin. 2010), p. 64.

62 *Ibid.*, pp. 65–6.

Chapter One

1 White House, *Cyberspace Policy Review: Assuring a Trusted and Resilient Information and Communications Infrastructure* (Washington DC: US Government Printing Office, 2009), p. iii.

2 Cabinet Office, *Cyber Security Strategy of the United Kingdom: Safety, Security and Resilience in Cyber Space* (Norwich: The Stationery Office, 2009), p. 7.

3 Public Safety Canada, *Canada's Cyber Security Strategy: For a Stronger and More Prosperous Canada* (Ottawa: Government of Canada Publications), p. 2.

4 Attorney-General's Department, *Cyber Security Strategy* (Canberra: Australian Government, 2009).

5 Susanna Paasonen, 'What Cyberspace? Traveling Concepts in Internet Research', in Gerard Goggin and Mark McLelland (eds), *Internationalizing Internet Studies: Beyond Anglophone Paradigms* (New York and Abingdon: Routledge, 2009), pp. 18–31.

6 William Gibson, interviewed in *No Maps for These Territories*, dir. Mark Neale, 89 min (Mark Neale Productions, 2000).

7 In *The Hacker Crackdown*, Sterling describes cyberspace as the 'place between the phones. The indefinite place out there, where the two of you, two human beings, actually meet and communicate'; this easily translates to the place between any networked electronic devices.

8 For an in-depth discussion of these issues, see Julie E. Cohen, 'Cyberspace As/And Space', *Columbia Law Review*, vol. 107, no. 1, January 2007, pp. 210–56.

9 Tom Boellstorff, *Coming of Age in Second Life: An Anthropologist Explores the Virtually Human* (Princeton, NJ and Oxford: Princeton University Press, 2008), p. 21.

10 Martin C. Libicki, *Conquest in Cyberspace: National Security and Information Warfare* (New York: Cambridge University Press, 2007), pp. 236–40. Libicki describes a fourth (pragmatic) layer but omits it from later work, e.g. Martin C. Libicki, *Cyberdeterrence and Cyberwar* (Santa Monica, CA: RAND Corporation, 2009), pp. 12–13.

11 John Urry, *Global Complexity* (Cambridge: Polity, 2003), p. 60.

12 *Ibid.*

13 Paul Virilio, *Speed and Politics: An Essay on Dromology*, tr. Mark Polizzoti, 2nd. rev. edn. (Los Angeles, CA: Semiotext(e), 2006).

14 Bertrand Russell, *Power: A New Social Analysis* (London and New York: Routledge, 2004), p. 23.

15 Andrew Hoskins and Ben O'Loughlin, *War and Media: The Emergence of Diffused*

War (Malden, MA, and Cambridge: Polity, 2010), p. 2.

16   Ellen Nakashima, 'Pentagon's Dismantling of Saudi–CIA Web Site Illustrates Need for Clearer Policies', *Washington Post*, 19 March 2010.

17   *The Guardian* newspaper maintains a useful archive of Anonymous-related material, http://www.guardian.co.uk/technology/anonymous.

18   On how this affects political dynamics, see David Resnick, 'Politics on the Internet: The Normalization of Cyberspace', in Chris Toulouse and Timothy W. Luke (eds), *The Politics of Cyberspace* (New York and London: Routledge, 1998), pp. 48–68.

19   Michael Barnett and Raymond Duvall, 'Power in International Politics', *International Organization*, vol. 59, no. 1, Winter 2005, pp. 39–75. See also Michael Barnett and Raymond Duvall, 'Power in Global Governance', in Michael Barnett and Raymond Duvall (eds.), *Power in Global Governance* (Cambridge: Cambridge University Press, 2005), pp. 1–32.

20   Max Weber, 'Class, Status, Party', in Hans Gerth and C. Wright Mills (eds), *From Max Weber: Essays in Sociology* (London: Routledge and Kegan Paul, 1948), p. 180.

21   Robert Dahl, 'The Concept of Power', *Behavioral Science*, vol. 2, no. 3, July 1957, pp. 201–15.

22   Lawrence Freedman, *The Transformation of Strategic Affairs*, Adelphi paper 379 (Abingdon: Routledge for the IISS, 2006), pp. 8–9.

23   William Mitchell, *Winged Defense: The Development and Possibilities of Modern Air Power – Economic and Military* (New York: Dover Publications, 1988), p. xii.

24   For example, Ranulph Glanville, 'A (Cybernetic) Musing: The State of Cybernetics', *Cybernetics & Human Knowing*, vol. 7, nos. 2–3, 2000, pp. 151–9; Ryan Singel, 'Check the Hype – There's No Such Thing as Cyber', *Wired*, 26 March 2010, http://www.wired.com/threatlevel/2010/03/cyber-hype/.

25   Tim Jordan, *Cyberpower: The Culture and Politics of Cyberspace and the Internet* (London and New York: Routledge, 1999), p. 3.

26   Daniel T. Kuehl, 'From Cyberspace to Cyberpower: Defining the Problem', in Franklin D. Kramer, Stuart H. Starr and Larry K. Wentz (eds), *Cyberpower and National Security* (Washington DC: National Defense University Press and Potomac Books, Inc., 2009), pp. 41–2.

27   Carl von Clausewitz, *On War*, edited and translated by Michael Howard and Peter Paret (Princeton, NJ: Princeton University Press, 1976), p. 75.

28   Our discussion is strongly informed by Barnett and Duvall, 'Power in International Politics', although for reasons of brevity we do not deploy their full and exhaustive argument here.

29   A solid introduction to 'cyber conflict' is Athina Karatzogianni, 'Introduction: New Media and the Reconfiguration of Power in Global Politics', in Athina Karatzogianni (ed.), *Cyber Conflict and Global Politics* (London and New York: Routledge, 2009), pp. 1–10.

30   Quoted by Nate Anderson in 'Anonymous vs HB Gary: The Aftermath', *ars technica* (February 2011), http://arstechnica.com/tech-policy/news/2011/02/anonymous-vs-hbgary-the-aftermath.ars.

31   *Ibid.*

32   Sean Lawson, *Beyond Cyber Doom: Cyber Attack Scenarios and the Evidence of History*, Working Paper no. 10–77

(Arlington, VA: Mercatus Center, George Mason University, 2011), http://mercatus.org/publication/beyond-cyber-doom. See also, Myriam Dunn Cavelty, *Cyber-Security and Threat Politics: US Efforts to Secure the Information Age* (London and New York: Routledge, 2008).

33 *Cyber Security Strategy of the United Kingdom*, p. 4.

34 Other factors also contribute to the difficulties of cyber deterrence, such as cyberspace's offence-dominant characteristics. See Libicki, *Cyberdeterrence and Cyberwar*, ch.3.

35 Barnett and Duvall, 'Power in International Politics', p. 51.

36 Nye, *Cyber Power*. Some of these activities are also discussed in our section on 'Productive Cyberpower'.

37 Milton L. Mueller, *Networks and States: The Global Politics of Internet Governance* (Cambridge, MA and London: the MIT Press, 2010), pp. 6off.

38 See, for example, White House, *International Strategy for Cyberspace: Prosperity, Security, and Openness in a Networked World*, May 2011, http://www.whitehouse.gov/sites/default/files/rss_viewer/international_strategy_for_cyberspace.pdf.

39 *Cyber Security Strategy of the United Kingdom*, p. 18.

40 Barnett and Duvall, 'Power in International Politics', pp. 52–5.

41 Fritz Machlup, *The Production and Distribution of Knowledge in the United States* (Princeton, NJ: Princeton University Press, 1962); Peter F. Drucker, *The Age of Discontinuity: Guidelines to Our Changing Society* (1969; London: Pan Books, 1971); Daniel Bell, *The Coming of the Post-Industrial Society: A Venture in Social Forecasting* (London: Heinemann Educational, 1974).

42 Manuel Castells, *The Rise of the Network Society* (1996; Malden, MA and Oxford: Blackwell, 2000), p. 21, fn31.

43 Christian Fuchs, *Internet and Society: Social Theory in the Information Age* (New York and Abingdon: Routledge, 2008).

44 *Ibid.* Fuchs reminds us that information economies have not dispensed with manufacturing entirely, as shown by the demand for hardware infrastructures to support them.

45 Most authors concede that networks of various forms are as old as mankind itself.

46 Manuel Castells, *The Internet Galaxy: Reflections on the Internet, Business, and Society* (Oxford: Oxford University Press, 2001), p. 138.

47 Castells, *Communication Power*, p. 120. This is similar to the concept of 'individual cyber-power', which develops as the fluidity of identity and relative social mobility of cyberspace allow for the generation of 'little pieces of power ... that individuals take up and possess, utilising them to impose their will ... for or against another avatar', Jordan, *Cyberpower*, p. 88.

48 Clarissa Rile Hayward, *De-Facing Power* (Cambridge: Cambridge University Press, 2000), p. 30, cited in Barnett and Duvall, 'Power in International Politics', p. 56.

49 Carsten F. Roennfeldt, 'Productive War: A Re-Conceptualisation of War', *Journal of Strategic Studies*, vol. 34, no. 1, 2011, pp. 39–62.

50 Helen Nissenbaum, 'Hackers and the Contested Ontology of Cyberspace', *New Media & Society*, vol. 6, no. 2, April 2004, pp. 195–217.

51 *Ibid.*, pp. 199, 204.

52 Luiza Ch. Savage, 'Julian Assange: The Man Who Exposed the

World', *Macleans*, 13 December 2010, http://www2.macleans.ca/2010/12/13/a-man-of-many-secrets/.

53 Lolita C. Baldor, 'Wanted: Computer Hackers ... To Help Government', Associated Press, 19 April 2009.

54 Duncan Gardham, 'Hackers Hired to Halt Attacks on Britain by Cyber Terrorists', *Daily Telegraph*, 26 June 2009.

55 The city of Fallujah was described as a 'rats' nest' of terrorist and insurgent activity by US generals and politicians keen to exert 'full-spectrum dominance' over a population it perceived to be resisting its presence and frustrating its goals. See Stephen Graham, 'Remember Fallujah: Demonising Place, Constructing Atrocity', *Environment & Planning D:*
Society & Space, vol. 23, no. 1, 2005, pp. 1–10. For a balanced account of cyberspace and jihad, see Gary R. Bunt, *iMuslims: Rewiring the House of Islam* (London: Hurst &Company, 2009), pp. 177–241.

56 Roennfeldt, 'Productive War'.

57 A recent study concludes that hateful representations of the 'other' in online environments, in this case of Israelis and Palestinians, were 'much more similar than one would expect'; Adi Kuntsman, 'Webs of Hate in Diasporic Cyberspaces: The Gaza War in the Russian-Language Blogosphere', *Media, War & Conflict*, vol. 3, no. 3, December 2010, pp. 299–313.

58 Simon Cottle, *Mediatized Conflict* (Maidenhead: Open University Press, 2006).

Chapter Two

1 Arjun Appadurai, *Modernity at Large: Cultural Dimensions of Globalization* (Minneapolis, MN: University of Minnesota Press, 1996), p. 19.

2 Jean-Marie Guéhenno, *The End of the Nation-State*, trans. Victoria Elliott (1993; Minneapolis, MN: University of Minnesota Press, 1995).

3 Saskia Sassen, *Losing Control? Sovereignty in an Age of Globalization* (New York: Columbia University Press, 1996).

4 Martin Wolf, 'Globalisation and the State', *Financial Times*, 22 September 1995, quoted in Stephen J. Kobrin, 'The Architecture of Globalization: State Sovereignty in a Networked Global Economy', in John H. Dunning (ed.), *Governments, Globalization,*
and International Business (Oxford: Oxford University Press, 1997), pp. 147.

5 John Perry Barlow, 'A Declaration of the Independence of Cyberspace', in Peter Ludlow (ed.), *Crypto Anarchy, Cyberstates, and Pirate Utopias* (Cambridge, MA: the MIT Press, 2001), pp. 27–30.

6 See, for example, John Perry Barlow, lecture to the European Graduate School, Saas-Fee, Switzerland, 29 May 2006, http://www.egs.edu/faculty/john-perry-barlow/videos/independence-declaration-of-cyberspace/.

7 Jens Bartelson, *A Genealogy of Sovereignty* (Cambridge: Cambridge University Press, 1995).

8 F.H. Hinsley, *Sovereignty*, 2nd edn (Cambridge: Cambridge University Press, 1986).

9 Robert O. Keohane, 'Ironies of Sovereignty: The European Union and the United States', *Journal of Common Market Studies*, vol. 40, no. 4, November 2002, pp. 743–65.

10 Stephen D. Krasner, *Power, The State, and Sovereignty: Essays on International Relations* (London and New York: Routledge, 2009), p. xiii.

11 Robert O. Keohane, 'Sovereignty, Interdependence, and International Institutions', in Linda B. Miller and Michael Joseph Smith (eds), *Ideas and Ideals: Essays in Honor of Stanley Hoffman* (Boulder, CO: Westview Press, 1993), cited in Kobrin, 'The Architecture of Globalization', p. 155.

12 Stephen D. Krasner, *Sovereignty: Organized Hypocrisy* (Princeton, NJ: Princeton University Press, 1999).

13 *Ibid.*

14 *Ibid.*, pp. 14–20. Krasner correctly notes that it is not states who make decisions in international politics but the rulers of states (p. 7) and our comments should be read with this in mind.

15 We exclude from our analysis online attempts by, for example, Palestinians and Israelis to denigrate the sovereign status of the others' countries, or of other similar campaigns.

16 For information on Sealand, see http://www.sealandgov.org/.

17 Simson Garfinkel, 'Welcome to Sealand. Now Bugger Off', *Wired*, vol. 8, no. 7, July 2000, http://www.wired.com/wired/archive/8.07/haven.html; 'Piratebay's "Sovereign Ambitions" Blasted', *The Register*, 17 January 2007, http://www.theregister.co.uk/2007/01/17/piratebay_sealand_nationhood/.

18 Two foundational texts of this viewpoint are: David R. Johnson and David Post, 'Law and Borders – The Rise of Law in Cyberspace', *Stanford Law Review*, vol. 48, no. 5, May 1996, pp. 1,367–1,402; Barlow, 'A Declaration of the Independence of Cyberspace'.

19 Timothy S. Wu, 'Cyberspace Sovereignty? The Internet and the International System', *Harvard Journal of Law & Technology*, vol. 10, no. 3, Summer 1997, pp. 648–9.

20 In 2010, press reports that the US was proposing an ambassador 'for' or 'to' cyberspace in the International Cyberspace and Cybersecurity Coordination Act of 2010 (S.3193) gave the false impression that the US thereby recognised cyberspace as a legal sovereign entity. In fact, the proposed post was for a State Department Coordinator for Cyberspace and Cybersecurity Issues, responsible for representing US cyberspace policy overseas and holding the rank of Ambassador at Large. This in no way implied the de facto or de jure recognition of cyberspace legal sovereignty. See Siobhan Gorman, 'US Aims to Bolster Overseas Fight Against Cybercrime', *Wall Street Journal*, 23 March 2010.

21 Krasner, *Sovereignty*, p. 20.

22 Richard Stiennon, *Surviving Cyberwar* (Lanham, MD: Government Institutes, 2010), pp. 85–104.

23 William J. Broad, John Markoff, and David E. Sanger, 'Israel Tests Called Crucial in Iran Nuclear Setback', *New York Times*, 16 January 2011.

24 Council of Europe, *Convention on Cybercrime*, 2001, http://conventions.coe.int/treaty/en/treaties/html/185.htm.

25 Ian Brown, Lilian Edwards and Christopher Marsden, 'Information

Security and Cybercrime', in Lilian Edwards and Charlotte Waelde (eds), *Law and the Internet*, 3rd edn (Oxford: Hart Publishing, 2009), pp. 671–92.

26 John Markoff and Andrew E. Kramer, 'US and Russia Differ on Treaty for Cyberspace', *New York Times*, 28 June 2009.

27 Jay P. Kesan and Carol M. Hayes, 'Thinking Through Active Defense in Cyberspace', *Proceedings of the Workshop on Deterring Cyberattacks: Informing Strategies and Developing Options* (Washington DC: National Academies Press, 2010), pp. 327–42.

28 Krasner, *Sovereignty*, p. 11.

29 Cabinet Office, *Cyber Security Strategy*, p. 17.

30 *Ibid.*, pp. 19–20.

31 Ronald Deibert, John Palfrey, Rafal Rohozinski and Jonathan Zittrain (eds), *Access Denied: The Practice and Policy of Global Internet Filtering* (Cambridge, MA and London: The MIT Press, 2008), and *Access Controlled: The Shaping of Power, Rights, and Rule in Cyberspace* (Cambridge, MA and London: The MIT Press, 2010).

32 Deibert *et al.*, *Access Controlled*, pp. 22–8.

33 Josh Goldstein, *The Role of Digital Networked Technologies in the Ukrainian Orange Revolution* (Cambridge, MA: Berkman Center for Internet and Society, Harvard University, 2007), http://cyber.law.harvard.edu/publications/2007/The_Role_of_Digital_Networked_Technologies_in_the_Ukranian_Orange_Revolution; Bibi van der Zee, 'Twitter Triumphs', *Index on Censorship*, vol. 38, no. 4, November 2009, pp. 97–102.

34 Evgeny Morozov, *The Net Delusion: The Dark Side of Internet Freedom* (New York: PublicAffairs, 2011).

35 First-generation controls exist, such as British Telecom's Cleanfeed filtering system, which is used to prevent access to child sexual abuse imagery, but are not, to the best of our knowledge, routinely used to suppress political material in countries like the US and the UK.

36 Duncan Gardham, Gordon Rayner, and John Bingham, 'Shut Down Videos of Hate on YouTube', *Daily Telegraph*, 3 November 2010. The Arabic-language *Al Arabiya* news channel has dubbed al-Awlaki 'the bin Laden of the Internet'; Aamer Madhani, 'What Makes Cleric Al-Awlaki So Dangerous', *USA Today*, 25 August 2010.

37 Cabinet Office, *The United Kingdom's Strategy for Countering International Terrorism* (Norwich: The Stationery Office, 2009), p. 153.

38 One widely-publicised study is David Stevens, *Estimating Network Size and Tracking Information Dissemination Amongst Islamic Blogs* (London: Home Office, 2010).

39 Cabinet Office, *UK Strategy for Countering International Terrorism*, p. 153.

40 *Securing Britain in an Age of Uncertainty: The Strategic Defence and Security Review* (Norwich: The Stationery Office, 2010), p. 44.

41 Timothy W. Luke, 'Simulated Sovereignty, Telematic Territoriality: The Political Economy of Cyberspace', paper presented to the conference, 'Culture and Identity: City, Nation, World; Second Theory, Culture and Society Conference', Berlin, 10–14 August 1995.

42 Krasner, *Sovereignty*, p. 12.

43 This is attributed to Tim May, former chief scientist at Intel and co-founder

of the Cypherpunks mailing list, c.1996, and is widely quoted online.

44 Krasner, *Sovereignty*, p. 13.

45 The characterisation of modern Islamist terrorism as a 'global insurgency' is partly predicated on the ability of al-Qaeda and its ilk to mobilise political support and actions globally through the use of communications technologies like the Internet. See John Mackinlay, *The Insurgent Archipelago: From Mao to Bin Laden* (London: Hurst and Company, 2009).

46 Akil N. Awan, 'Virtual Jihadist Media: Function, Legitimacy and Radicalizing Efficacy', *European Journal of Cultural Studies*, vol. 10, no. 3, August 2007, pp. 389–408.

47 Hillary Clinton, 'Remarks on Internet Freedom', speech, Washington DC; 21 January 2010; John Kampfner, 'What Next After Wikileaks?', *Guardian*, 17 January 2011.

48 Hence calls for the Internet to be 're-engineered'; Mike McConnell, 'To Win the Cyber-War, Look to the Cold War', *Washington Post*, 28 February 2010.

49 'A Virtual Counter-Revolution', *The Economist*, 4 September 2010. As this article points out, other forms of balkanisation are also occurring, most notably due to IT companies 'building their own digital territories' and the recent decision to allow non-English script domain names, thereby fomenting linguistic divergences within the domain-name system.

50 Masashi Crete-Nishihata and Jillian C. York, 'Egypt's Internet Blackout: Extreme Example of Just-in-Time Blocking', *OpenNet Initiative* (28 January 2011), http://opennet.net/blog/2011/01/egypt%E2%80%99s-Internet-blackout-extreme-example-just-time-blocking.

51 Stephen W. Korns, 'Cyber Operations: The New Balance', *Joint Forces Quarterly*, vol. 54, no. 3, Fall 2009, pp. 97–102.

52 Stephen D. Krasner, 'Abiding Sovereignty', *International Political Science Review*, vol. 22, no. 3, July 2001, pp. 229–51.

53 Such sovereignty-pooling exercises may actually enhance the opportunities for democratic governance and control, provided they are subject to democratic accountability; Robert O. Keohane, Stephen Macedo and Andrew Moravcsik, 'Democracy-Enhancing Multilateralism', *International Organization*, vol. 63, no. 1, Winter 2009, pp. 1–31.

Chapter Three

1 See, for example, Tyler Cowen, *The Age of the Infovore* (London: Penguin, 2011); or Clay Shirky, *Here Comes Everybody* (London: Penguin, 2009); on the effect of the Internet on brains see Nicholas Carr, 'Is Google Making us Stupid?', *The Atlantic* (July/August 2008).

2 Marshall Poe, *A History of Communications* (Cambridge: Cambridge University Press, 2010).

3 Quoted in Michael S. Sherry, *The Rise of American Air Power* (New Haven, CT: Yale University Press, 1987), p. 9.

4   Qiao Liang and Wang Xiangsui, *Unrestricted Warfare* (Beijing: PLA Literature and Arts Publishing House, February 1999), pp. 129 & 199.

5   See Fred Halliday, *The World at 2000: Perils and Promises* (London: Palgrave, 2000), pp. 15–18, for a discussion of the dangers of 'presentism'.

6   See Hew Strachan, 'The Changing Character of War', Europaeum Lecture delivered at the Graduate Institute of International Relations (Geneva, 9 November 2006) http://www.europaeum.org/files/publications/pamphlets/HewStrachan.pdf; also, Strachan, *On War, A Biography* (London: Atlantic Books, 2007).

7   See Richard Ned Lebow, *A Cultural Theory of International Relations* (Cambridge: Cambridge University Press 2008) for a discussion of the role of fear, honour and self-interest on state behaviour over the years.

8   Rupert Smith, *The Utility of Force* (London: Allen Lane, 2005), p. 1.

9   Norman Angell, *The Great Illusion* (London: William Heinemann, 1910), p. 222.

10 Kalevi Holsti, *The State, War and the State of War* (Cambridge: Cambridge University Press, 1996), p. 22.

11 Hew Strachan, 'One War, Joint Warfare', *RUSI Journal*, vol. 154, no. 4, 2009, p. 22.

12 Brian Bond, *The Pursuit of Victory* (Oxford: Oxford University Press, 1996). It needs to be said, however, that this is a euro-centric view: war does pay in places like Africa and major wars such as that between Iraq in Iran in the 1980s have been fought. See Mary Kaldor, *New and Old Wars* (Cambridge: Polity, 2006), and Mats Berdal and David Malone, *Greed & Grievance* (Boulder, CO: Lynne Reiner, 2000).

13 Powell is quoted in 'Ideas and Consequences', *The Atlantic* magazine, October 2007, http://www.theatlantic.com/magazine/archive/2007/10/ideas-and-consequences/6193/; Michael Howard, 'A Long War', *Survival*, vol. 48, no. 4, Winter 2006–07, p. 13.

14 Angell, p. 298.

15 The poles of the debate may be seen in John Nagl's 'Let's Win the Wars We're In' and Gian P. Gentile's 'Let's Build an Army to Win All Wars', both in *Joint Force Quarterly*, no. 52, 1st quarter, 2009, pp. 20–26 & 27–33 respectively.

16 Frank G. Hoffman, *Conflict in the 21st Century: The Rise of Hybrid Wars* (Washington DC: Potomac Institute, 2007).

17 General Sir David Richards, 'Future Conflict and Its Prevention: People and the Information Age', International Institute for Strategic Studies, 18 January 2010, http://www.iiss.org/recent-key-addresses/general-sir-david-richards-address/.

18 Castells, *Communication Power*, p. 49.

19 Richards, 'Future Conflict...'.

20 Smith, pp. 16–18 & 371–2.

21 Barry Buzan, Ole Waever and Jaap de Wilde, *Security: A New Framework for Analysis* (Boulder, CO: Lynne Rienner, 1998).

22 BBC, *The Virtual Revolution*, Episode 2 'The Enemy of the State?', aired on BBC2, 6 February 2010, http://www.bbc.co.uk/programmes/b00n4j0r.

23 Sherry, p. 23.

24 J.F.C. Fuller, *The Reformation of War* (London: Hutchinson, 1923), http://www.archive.org/stream/reformationofwaroofulluoft/reformationofwaroofulluoft_djvu.txt.

25 The full text of the Baldwin House of Commons speech from 10 November 1932 may be found on the 'Airminded' blog, http://airminded.org/2007/11/10/

the-bomber-will-always-get-through/; Baldwin was echoing the claims of the Italian air power theorist Giulio Douhet, *The Command of the Air*, trans. Dino Ferrari (New York: Faber and Faber, 1942).

26 Charles Stross, *Singularity Sky* (London: Ace Books, 2003); also Paul Virilio, *Information Bomb* (London: Verso, 2005).

27 See David Betz, 'Kuang Grade Mark 11 Targets Iranian Computers', *Kings of War* (London: Department of War Studies, King's College London, 28 September 2010), http://kingsofwar. org.uk/2010/09/kuang-grade-mark-11-targets-iranian-nuclear-facilities/.

28 Quoted in Sherry, p. 9.

29 *Ibid.*, p. 30.

30 *Ibid.*, p. 24.

31 Fuller, p. 150.

32 Sherry, p. 26.

33 *Ibid.*, p. 26.

34 The White House, *National Strategy to Secure Cyberspace* (Washington DC: 2003), p. vii, http://www.dhs.gov/ xlibrary/assets/National_Cyberspace_ Strategy.pdf.

35 Sherry, p. 41

36 Quoted in 'The Necessity of Student Exchanges', *Inside Higher Ed*, 17 November 2005, http://www. insidehighered.com/news/2005/11/17/ exchange.

37 Sherry, p. 30.

38 Eliot Cohen, 'The Mystique of US Air Power', *Foreign Affairs*, vol. 73, no. 1, January/ February 1994, p. 109.

39 See *Cyberspace Operations*, United States Air Force Doctrine Document 3–12 (15 July 2010), p. 10, http:// www.e-publishing.af.mil/shared/ media/epubs/afdd3-12.pdf.

40 For a cogent example of such thinking see Benjamin Lambeth 'Airpower,

Spacepower and Cyberpower', *Joint Force Quarterly*, no. 60, 1st quarter, 2011, pp. 47–53.

41 Daniel Byman and Matthew Waxman, 'Kosovo and the Great Air Power Debate', *International Security*, vol. 24, no. 4, Spring 2000, pp. 5–38.

42 In Chapter 8, 'Information Systems Security', in Joint Security Commission, *Redefining Security* (Washington DC, 28 February 1994), http://www.fas.org/ sgp/library/jsc/chap8.html.

43 H.R. McMaster, 'Learning from Contemporary Conflicts to Prepare for Future War', *Orbis*, vol. 52, no. 4, 2008, pp. 564–84.

44 David Betz, 'The More You Know, the Less You Understand: The Problem with Information Warfare', *Journal of Strategic Studies*, vol. 29, no. 3, 2006, pp. 505–34.

45 On the end of history see Francis Fukuyama, *The End of History and the Last Man* (New York: The Free Press, 1992); on advances in military capability see William Owens, *Lifting the Fog of War* (Baltimore, MD: Johns Hopkins University Press, 2000).

46 The title of the US Army Capstone Concept, *Operational Adaptation: Operating Under Conditions of Uncertainty and Complexity in an Era of Persistent Conflict*, TRADOC Pam 525-3-0 (21 December 2009) clearly reveals this anxiety.

47 John Robb, *Brave New War* (Hoboken, NJ: John Wiley and Sons, 2007).

48 James Adams, *The Next World War* (New York: Simon and Schuster, 1998), p. 313.

49 Lambeth, p. 51.

50 Quoted in Helen Nissenbaum, 'Where Computer Security Meets National Security' in Jack M. Balkin *et al.* (eds),

Cybercrime (New York: New York University Press, 2007), p. 71.

51 Adams, p. 16.

52 Liddell-Hart, Strategy; Sun Tzu, The Art of War, Lionel Giles trans. (London: Luzac and Co., 1910).

53 Richard Clarke, Cyber War (New York, HarperCollins, 2010), pp. 67–68.

54 Clausewitz, p. 83.

55 Clarke, p. 148.

56 Libicki, Conquest in Cyberspace, pp. 3 & 39.

57 Clausewitz, p. 111.

58 Libicki, Conquest in Cyberspace, pp. 291–306.

59 Clarke, p. 149.

60 US Air Force, Cyberspace Operations, p. 10.

61 In business, a 'pure play' is a company which has a single business focus, for example Coca-Cola, which retails only beverages.

62 John Arquila and David Ronfeldt, 'Cyberwar is Coming', in Arquila and Ronfeldt (eds), In Athena's Camp: Preparing for Conflict in the Information Age (Santa Monica, CA: RAND, 1997), p. 23.

63 Iain Lobban, Director of UK Government Communications Headquarters, Speech at the International Institute for Strategic Studies, 12 October 2010.

64 See David Betz, 'Keeping the Enemy out of your Harddrive', Parliamentary Brief (1 July 2011), http://www.parliamentarybrief.com/2010/10/keeping-the-enemy-out-of-your-hard-drive.

65 Clausewitz, p. 100.

Chapter Four

1 Quadrennial Defense Review, p. 8.

2 United States Department of Defence, National Defense Strategy (Washington DC: 2008), p. 16.

3 Walter Russell Mead, God and Gold (New York: Random House, 2007), p. 341.

4 Barry Posen, 'Command of the Commons: The Military Foundation of US Hegemony', International Security, vol. 28, no. 1, Summer 2003, p. 8.

5 Immanel Wallerstein, The Modern World-System, vol. I: Capitalist Agriculture and the Origins of the European World-Economy in the Sixteenth Century (New York: Academic Press, 1974), p. 233; in similar vein Michael Hardt and Antonio Negri, Empire (Cambridge, MA: Harvard University Press, 2000).

6 A Strong Britain in an Age of Uncertainty, p. 21.

7 Philip Bobbitt, The Shield of Achilles (London: Allen Lane, 2002).

8 Alfred Thayer Mahan, The Influence of Sea Power Upon History, 1600–1783 (New York: Dover Publications, 1987).

9 Tim Jordan and Paul Taylor have done some of the best work on this issue; see Hacktivism and Cyberwars: Rebels with a Cause? (London: Routledge, 2004).

10 Harold Lasswell, Politics: Who Gets What, When and How (New York: Whittlesey House, 1936).

11 William Blackstone, Commentaries on the Laws of England, Vol. 1 (New York: Collins and Co., 1827), p. 1.

12 Fareed Zakaria, The Post-American World and the Rise of the Rest (London: Penguin Books, 2008).

13 Julian Corbett, *Some Principles of Maritime Strategy* (Annapolis, MD: Naval Institute Press, 1988), p. 57.

14 Frances Cairncross, *Death of Distance: How the Communications Revolution is Changing Our Lives* (Cambridge, MA: Harvard Business School Press, 2001).

15 Quoted in H. Peter Alesso and George F. Smith, *Patterns of Discovery* (Hoboken, NJ: John Wiley and Sons, 2008), p. 122.

16 James H. Mittelman, *Hyperconflict: Globalization and Insecurity* (Stanford, CA: Stanford University Press, 2010), p. 2.

17 Libicki, *Conquest in Cyberspace*, p. 6.

18 Clay Shirky, *Cognitive Surplus* (London: Allen Lane, 2010), p. 37.

19 Arquila and Ronfeldt, 'The Advent of Netwar' in Arquial and Ronfeldt (eds), *In Athena's Camp*, p. 275.

20 Susan J. Buck, *The Global Commons: An Introduction* (Washington DC: Island Press, 1998), pp. 5–6.

21 See Patrick Franzese, 'Sovereignty in Cyberspace: Can it Exist?', *Air Force Law Review*, vol. 64, 2009, pp. 14–17.

22 See Abe Denmark and James Mulvenon (eds), *Contested Commons* (Washington DC: Center for a New American Security, January 2010), p. 13.

23 See Strachan, 'One War, Joint Warfare'.

24 *Quadrennial Defense Review*, p. 37.

25 *Ibid.*

26 FM 3-24 *Counterinsurgency* (Washington, DC: Headquarters Department of the Army, 2006), p. 1–3.

27 See Neville Bolt and David Betz, *Propaganda of the Deed 2008: Understanding the Phenomenon*, Whitehall Paper (London: Royal United Services Institute, 2008).

28 Andrew Hoskins and Ben O'Loughlin, *Television and Terror* (Houndmills, Basingstoke: Palgrave Macmillan, 2009).

29 Paul Virilio, *Information Bomb* (London: Verso, 2005), p. 63.

30 Martin Libicki, 'What is Information Warfare?' *Strategic Forum 28*, May 1995; also Roger Molander, Andrew Riddile and Peter Wilson, 'Strategic Information Warfare: A New Face of War', *Parameters*, Autumn 1996, pp. 81–92.

31 Libicki, *Conquest in Cyberspace*, p. 37.

32 Denise Schmandt-Besserat, *Before Writing* (Austin, TX: University of Texas Press, 1998), pp. 158–61.

33 *Ibid.*, p. 192.

34 Carl Kaestle, 'The History of Literacy and the History of Readers', *Review of Research in Education*, vol. 12, 1985, p. 19.

35 Albert Borgmann, *Holding on to Reality* (Chicago, IL: University of Chicago Press, 1999).

36 Steven Livingston, 'Clarifying the CNN Effect', Shorenstein Centre, Harvard University, Research Paper R-18 (1997).

37 Andrew Mack, 'Why Big Nations Lose Small Wars', in Klaus Knorr (ed.), *Power Strategy and Security: A World Politics Reader* (Princeton, NJ: Princeton University Press, 1975), pp. 126–51; and Ivan Arreguin-Toft, *How the Weak Win Wars: A Theory of Asymmetric Conflict* (Cambridge: Cambridge University Press, 2005).

38 Jenkins initially voiced this theory in 1975 but has reprised it in *Will Terrorists Go Nuclear?* (Amherst, NY: Prometheus Books, 2008).

39 Margaret Thatcher, Speech to the American Bar Association, 15 July 1985, http://www.margaretthatcher.org/document/106096.

40 Shirky, *Cognitive Surplus*, p. 30.

41 Hoskins and O'Loughlin, *Television and Terror*, p. 192.

42 Clausewitz, p. 99.

43 Harold Lasswell, 'The Structure and Function of Communication in Society', in Lyman Bryson (ed.), *The Communication of Ideas* (New York: Harper and Row, 1948).

44 David Betz, 'The Virtual Dimension of Contemporary Insurgency and Counterinsurgency', *Small Wars and Insurgencies*, vol. 19, no. 4, 2008, pp. 513–43.

45 *Securing Britain in an Age of Uncertainty*, p. 16.

46 Marshall McLuhan, *Understanding Media* (Abingdon: Routledge, 2001), p. 370.

47 Although it also attracted a lot of heavyweight criticism. See Martin Van Creveld, 'It Will Continue to Conquer and Spread', *Contemporary Security Policy*, vol. 26, no. 2, 2005, pp. 229–32; Lawrence Freedman, 'War Evolves into the Fourth Generation: A Comment on Thomas X. Hammes', *Contemporary Security Policy*, vol. 26, no. 2, 2005, pp. 254–63; and Antulio Echevarria II, *Fourth Generation Warfare and Other Myths*, (Carlisle, PA: Strategic Studies Institute, November 2005).

48 T.X. Hammes, 'War Evolves into the Fourth Generation', *Contemporary Security Policy*, vol. 26, no. 2, 2005, p. 190.

49 *Ibid.*, p. 207.

50 Quoted in '2012 Olympics Could Face "Blended" Physical, Cyber Attack: Security Expert,' *Daily India*, 3 March 2010, http://www.dailyindia.com/show/366067.php.

51 Seymour Goodman, Jessica Kirk and Megan Kirk, 'Cyberspace as a Medium for Terrorists', *Technological Forecasting and Social Change*, vol. 74, no. 2, 2007, pp. 193–210.

52 Bruce Berkowitz, *The New Face of War: How War will be Fought in the 21st Century* (New York: The Free Press, 2003), p. 17.

53 John Robb, *Brave New War: The Next Stage of Terrorism and the End of Globalization* (London: Wiley, 2007).

54 Liang and Xiangsui, p. 116.

55 David Kilcullen, *The Accidental Guerrilla* (London: Hurst, 2009), p. 12.

56 Mark Duffield, 'War as a Network Enterprise: The New Security Terrain and its Implications', *Cultural Values*, vol. 6, nos 1&2, 2002, p. 158.

57 Kilcullen, p. 300.

58 Mackinlay, p. 6.

59 Emergent phenomena occur when simple entities operating in accordance with basic rules exhibit complex behaviours collectively. They tend to arise when a complex system possesses a high degree of diversity, organisation and connectivity. The complex behaviours of a collective are not easily deduced from behaviour of the individual entities that make it up. Examples of emergence are legion, including the flocking of birds and fish, ant colonies and slime moulds, traffic patterns, urban development, the stock market, weather systems and human consciousness. See J. Holland, *Emergence from Chaos to Order* (Oxford: Oxford University Press, 1998); also Stephen Johnson, *Emergence* (London: Penguin, 2001).

60 Mackinlay, p. 5.

61 Audrey Kurth Cronin, *Ending Terrorism*, Adelphi paper 394 (Abingdon: Routledge for the IISS, 2008), p. 53; also by same author 'Cyber-Mobilization: The New *Levee en Masse*', *Parameters*, Summer 2006, pp. 77–87.

62 See Betz, 'Virtual Dimension…'.

63 See Latour, *Reassembling the Social*.

64 Castells, *Communication Power*, p. 302.

65 Thomas Rid and Marc Hecker, 'Cracks in the Jihad', *The Wilson Quarterly*, Winter 2010, p. 47.

66 Corbett, pp. 87 & 102.

67 Castells, *Communication Power*, p. 301.

68 Sean Parson, 'Understanding the Ideology of the Earth Liberation Front', *Green Theory & Praxis: The Journal of Ecopedagogy*, vol. 4, no. 2, 2008.

69 Notes from Nowhere (eds), *We are Everywhere: The Irresistible Rise of Global Anti-Capitalism* (London: Verso, 2003), p. 16.

70 See David Betz, 'Cyber-subversives evolve at "netspeed"', *Kings of War*, 22 June 2011, http://www.kingsofwar.org.uk/2011/06cyber-subversives-evolve-at-netspeed.

71 See the post by David Betz and accompanying comments by Barratt Brown and others on 'Anonymous Spokesman Opens Nechayev's Tomb, Becomes Possessed', *Kings of War*, 14 March 2011, http://kingsofwar.org.uk/2011/03/anonymous-spokesman-opens-nechaevs-tomb-becomes-possessed/.

72 Ryan Singel, 'British Police Arrest 5 Men in Wikileaks-Anonymous Payback Attacks', *Wired* (27 January 2011), http://www.wired.com/threatlevel/2011/01/wikileaks-anonymous-arrest/.

73 Howard Rheingold, *Smart Mobs: The Next Social Revolution* (Cambridge, MA: Basic Books, 2002).

74 Spencer Ackerman, 'US has Secret Tools to Force Internet on Dictators', *Wired*, 7 February 2011, http://www.wired.com/dangerroom/2011/02/secret-tools-force-net/.

75 Rheingold, p. xii.

Conclusion

1 Susanne Huttner, 'The Internet Economy: Towards a Better Future', *OECD Observer*, no. 268, June 2008, http://www.oecdobserver.org/news/fullstory.php/aid/2330/.

2 'Number of Internet Users Worldwide Reaches 2 bln: UN', AFP, 26 January 2011.

3 '16bn Devices Online by 2020, Says Report', *Telegraph*, 30 October 2010, http://www.telegraph.co.uk/technology/Internet/8097488/16bn-devices-online-by-2020-says-report.html.

4 Fred Kaplan, *Wizards of Armageddon* (Stanford, CA: Stanford University Press, 1991).

5 John Perry Barlow, 'A Declaration of the Independence of Cyberspace', in Peter Ludlow (ed.), *Crypto Anarchy, Cyberstates, and Pirate Utopias* (Cambridge, MA: The MIT Press, 2001), pp. 27–30.

6 See http://www.bipartisanpolicy.org/events/cyber2010.

7 Cronin, 'Cyber-Mobilization...'.

8 BBC, *The Age of Uncertainty*, John Kenneth Galbraith and Andre Deutsch (1977).

9 Joshua Cooper Ramo, *The Age of the Unthinkable* (New York: Little Brown, 2009).

10 Oswald Spengler, *The Decline of the West*, 2 vols, trans. Charles Francis Atkinson (New York: Alfred A. Knopf, 1922).

11 Libicki, *Conquest in Cyberspace*, p. 55.

12 George Orwell, 'You and the Atom Bomb', *Tribune*, 19 October 1945.

13 William Broad, John Markoff and David Sanger, 'Israeli Test on Worm Called Crucial in Iran Nuclear Delay', *New York Times*, 15 January 2011, http://www.nytimes.com/2011/01/16/world/middleeast/16stuxnet.html.

14 Stephen Biddle, *Military Power* (Princeton, NJ: Princeton University Press, 2004).

15 William H. McNeill, *The Pursuit of Power* (Chicago, IL: Chicago University Press, 1984).

16 Betz, 'The More You Know…', p. 510.

17 John Dewey, *The Public and Its Problems* (New York: Holt, 1927), p. 34.

18 Dewey, pp. 33–4.

19 Joseph Schumpeter, *Capitalism, Socialism and Democracy* (New York: HarperPerennial, 1976).

20 Richard Clarke, 'Software Power: Cyber warfare is the risky new frontline', Harvard University Belfer Center 'Power and Policy' blog, 7 February 2011, http://belfercenter.ksg.harvard.edu/power/2011/02/07/software-power-cyber-warfare-is-the-risky-new-frontline/.

21 See Janice Thomson, *Mercenaries, Pirates and Sovereigns* (Princeton, NJ: Princeton University Press, 1994).

22 William Hague, 'Security and Freedom in the Cyber-Age', speech by the UK Foreign Secretary to the Munich Security Conference, 4 February, 2011, http://www.fco.gov.uk/en/news/latest-news/?id=545077882&view=Speech.

23 Bruce Sterling interview on 'Blast Shack' about WikiLeaks, 22 December 2010, http://www.webstock.org.nz/blog/2010/the-blast-shack/.

24 Marc Sageman, *Understanding Terror Networks* (Philadelphia, PA: University of Philadelphia Press, 2004) *Leaderless Jihad: Terror Networks in the Twenty-First Century* (Philadelphia, PA: University of Philadelphia Press, 2008).

25 Sterling, 'Blast Shack' interview.

26 Libicki, *Conquest in Cyberspace*, p. 35.

27 Castells, *Communication Power*, p. 39.

28 *Ibid.*

29 *Ibid.*, p. 42.

⌐IISS ADELPHI BOOKS

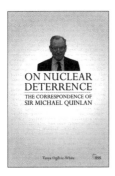

ADELPHI 421–3

On Nuclear Deterrence:
The Correspondence of
Sir Michael Quinlan

Tanya Ogilvie-White

Hardback: ISBN 978-0-415-69650-0
Paperback: ISBN 978-0-415-52165-9

ADELPHI 420

**Yemen and the Politics of
Permanent Crisis**

Sarah Phillips

ISBN 978-0-415-69574-9

ADELPHI 418–9

No Exit: North Korea,
Nuclear Weapons and
International Security

Jonathan D. Pollack

ISBN 978-0-415-67083-8

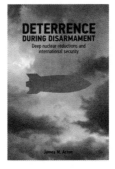

ADELPHI 417

**Deterrence During
Disarmament:** Deep Nuclear
Reductions and International
Security

James M. Acton

ISBN 978-0-415-66989-4

For credit card orders call **+44 (0) 1264 343 071**
or e-mail **book.orders@tandf.co.uk**
Orders can also be placed at **www.iiss.org**

Routledge
Taylor & Francis Group

Adelphi books are published eight times a year by Routledge Journals, an imprint of Taylor & Francis, 4 Park Square, Milton Park, Abingdon, Oxfordshire OX14 4RN, UK.

A subscription to the institution print edition, ISSN 1944-5571, includes free access for any number of concurrent users across a local area network to the online edition, ISSN 1944-558X

2012 Annual Adelphi Subscription Rates			
Institution	£525	$924 USD	€777
Individual	£239	$407 USD	€324
Online only	£473	$832 USD	€699

Dollar rates apply to subscribers outside Europe. Euro rates apply to all subscribers in Europe except the UK and the Republic of Ireland where the pound sterling price applies. All subscriptions are payable in advance and all rates include postage. Journals are sent by air to the USA, Canada, Mexico, India, Japan and Australasia. Subscriptions are entered on an annual basis, i.e. January to December. Payment may be made by sterling cheque, dollar cheque, international money order, National Giro, or credit card (Amex, Visa, Mastercard).

For more information, visit our website: **http://www.informaworld.com/ adelphipapers.**

For a complete and up-to-date guide to Taylor & Francis journals and books publishing programmes, and details of advertising in our journals, visit our website: **http://www.informaworld.com.**

Ordering information:
USA/Canada: Taylor & Francis Inc., Journals Department, 325 Chestnut Street, 8th Floor, Philadelphia, PA 19106, USA. **UK/Europe/Rest of World:** Routledge Journals, T&F Customer Services, T&F Informa UK Ltd., Sheepen Place, Colchester, Essex, CO3 3LP, UK.

Advertising enquiries to:
USA/Canada: The Advertising Manager, Taylor & Francis Inc., 325 Chestnut Street, 8th Floor, Philadelphia, PA 19106, USA. Tel: +1 (800) 354 1420. Fax: +1 (215) 625 2940.

UK/Europe/Rest of World: The Advertising Manager, Routledge Journals, Taylor & Francis, 4 Park Square, Milton Park, Abingdon, Oxfordshire OX14 4RN, UK. Tel: +44 (0) 20 7017 6000. Fax: +44 (0) 20 7017 6336.

The print edition of this journal is printed on ANSI conforming acid-free paper by Bell & Bain, Glasgow, UK.